A Case of Brilliance

A Case of Brilliance

To Arthur—
In Christ's love,
Becky Hein

Rebecca Lange Hein

To order additional copies of this book, contact:
Xlibris Corporation
1-888-7-XLIBRIS
www.Xlibris.com
Orders@Xlibris.com

To Ellis, Annette, and Lewis,
for being the brains of the operation.

Thousands of geniuses live and die undiscovered—either by themselves or by others.

Mark Twain

Contents

FOREWORD

The book you are about to read is one that I would have liked to have twenty-five years ago when my closest friend and I were raising our extraordinarily gifted sons with little access to information about unusual giftedness or about the personal reality of parenting such children. We had one book to give us a sense of community, a sense that we were not the first, not the only people confronting such problems, and some ideas about how to proceed— Audrey Grost's *Genius in Residence.* That book is long out of print.

Today there is much more written about the unique needs of children at the highest ranges of intelligence. There are both private and public internet lists for parents of profoundly gifted children, where they can share their experiences online. But even in a world where so much more information is available and it is possible to interact with other parents, most still experience a sense of aloneness, a sense of being forced almost every day to venture into unknown territory where any misstep seems likely to harm their children. Those outside that very small loop—from the teachers who find such children in their classroom, to the extended families of the children and parents, from pediatricians to scout masters to little league coaches and music teachers— find it hard to understand both the children's needs and the parents' daily reality. It is difficult for outsiders to grasp the full impact of being so far from the norms on which most of society is based. This book can provide a way into the experience of the profoundly gifted for anyone who has reason to be interested.

It is said that the way to tell a story that is most universal is to tell one that is absolutely specific. This is such a story. Rebecca Hein is not giving advice about parenting or teaching, not telling the reader about what profoundly gifted children are like. She is telling one very specific story, the story of her family, of her children, her husband and herself as they struggle to discover who they are and what is required of them to live fully in the world. The early part of the book is full of the confusion and doubts that most parents of brilliant children encounter. Virtually every such family finds itself reinventing the wheel, learning by trial and error what no one has codified (perhaps no one can) about raising such complex and asynchronous children. (The term "asynchronous" refers to the fact that the profoundly gifted are out of sync externally—with the expectations of a world built around norms—and also internally, as the many aspects of their development—intellectual, social, emotional, moral/spiritual and physical—move along separate and often quite different trajectories.)

Through the medium of music, Rebecca Hein

encountered and began to deal with her children's differences. The book details with great clarity the discoveries this mother made as she worked to find ways to teach the cello to her children in a way that fit their extraordinary learning speed, breadth and depth. Families who don't share the Hein's musical milieu will nevertheless recognize the frustrations, the breakthroughs and the step by step learning about the needs of exceptionally brilliant minds with a rage to learn.

A critical part of the journey this story describes is the discovery, not just of the asynchrony of the children, but of the asynchrony of the parents. Parents of profoundly gifted children seldom begin with a clear sense of their own extraordinary intelligence. Their personal journey of discovery must be undertaken at the same time they are struggling to figure out what their children's needs are and how to meet them. This aspect of the book, told with both passion and humility, may be among the most valuable, especially to women who still find it difficult to recognize or acknowledge the extent of their own gifts.

Each gifted reader's personal story will be different. And yet each will find in these pages a comforting familiarity. The profoundly gifted are rare in the human population. Finding community is not easy. This book is a step in that direction, reminding readers that, however unusual they may be, they are not alone.

Stephanie S. Tolan

Co-author of *Guiding the Gifted Child*, author of "Is It a Cheetah?" and other articles about the needs of the gifted.

www.stephanietolan.com

AUTHOR'S NOTE

When I began to learn about extreme intelligence, my thoughts were dominated by one word: "genius." However, as I talked with others about the issues surrounding this topic, I gradually realized that I'd been oblivious to the cultural connotations of that label.

As with a specific IQ number, the word genius creates expectations, even stereotypes, about those who possess it. The most common, and surely the most unfair (particularly to children), is the myth that high intelligence is obvious, and always develops into visible, specific achievements. While this can sometimes be true, it can also become an invasion of privacy. All people, including the most intelligent, have the right to live free of others' expectations, especially when those expectations are based on false assumptions and misinformation.

The experts (Silverman 1995) have stated that "there is so little known about this population [the most highly gifted] that it is critical to gather and share as much information as possible . . ." Therefore, the rest of us should take heed and choose our remarks carefully. When I first heard the term "profoundly gifted," it struck me as an accurate description of my family's situation; more subtle and less loaded than genius.

As my education about extreme intelligence evolved, I began to substitute "profoundly gifted" for "genius," both in my thoughts and on paper. I made this substitution because I wanted the reader, as well as myself, to participate in the shift of thought that happens when we begin to see gifted people as whole beings rather than just a set of phenomenal abilities.

ACKNOWLEDGEMENTS

Many people contributed their time and expertise to the development and completion of this book. I'm grateful to them all.

Ron Kenner edited the manuscript, and in the process became my writing teacher, mentor, and friend. Others who helped with earlier versions of the manuscript include Kiesa Kay and Jeanne Spawn. Dr. Linda Silverman granted permission to quote from her writings, and also took time out of her busy schedule, not once, but often, to discuss with me issues relating to giftedness. Annette Revel Sheely was always willing to answer my questions about the profoundly gifted. Lee Ann Powell of the Gifted Development Center saved me much time by helping to locate several references. Stephanie Tolan generously made room in her own schedule of writing to read the entire manuscript and write the Foreword. Deirdre Lovecky and the *Roeper Review* granted permission to quote at length from the article, "Exceptionally Gifted Children: Different Minds."

Those who shared their time and computer skills—saving me countless headaches—include Eric Unruh, who generated the musical examples, Jeremy Moyle, who was always on call when I got tangled in the intricacies of word processing, and my husband, Ellis, whose patience never flagged, no matter how often I yelled for help.

Ellis also listened to every draft of every chapter of this book. Sometimes when I was reading to him early in the morning, our children, Annette and Lewis, were tiptoeing around the kitchen, getting breakfast ready, providing both practical help and further inspiration.

INTRODUCTION

Our nation is plagued with societal, environmental, and fiscal problems, and what is our strategy? Do we search for our most brilliant young people, to nurture them and support their development from an early age, knowing that we need big minds to solve our big problems? Sadly, we do not. Most public schools have no official procedure for identifying gifted students, much less educating them.

The prevailing myth is that gifted children don't need help. In reality, the opposite is true. But this book is not about the failure of the public schools to serve our gifted. It is about success: the triumph of reality over denial, of education over ignorance.

Mine was both the denial and the ignorance. When our first child began doing amazing things at an early age, we could tell she was gifted but I refused to believe the full evidence of my eyes and ears. It was just too much—some of it downright unbelievable. It was easy to disbelieve the nearly impossible, so I did. I was helped in my ignorance by the general lack of societal concern for the gifted. I learned from library books that our daughter's developmental milestones—which we had suspected for some time—were accelerated. I also discovered something I had dimly known: that we couldn't expect any serious help from the public schools in either assessing or serving her educational needs. But there my learning about the gifted stopped.

Many of my deepest assumptions about giftedness were false, but I was too ill-informed to realize it. Probably no amount of reading could have convinced me then that our daughter needed testing, and that my husband and I needed expert advice. *Why?* I thought. *What's the point of knowing her IQ? We know she's bright—that's all we need to know. Besides, everybody knows that IQ tests aren't an accurate measure of intelligence.*

But I was wrong on all counts. It was critically important to learn her IQ and to seek the advice of experts. The decision to do so has changed my whole life, and now I am on a mission to reach other parents, and to write the book that I looked for on the shelves of my public library but was unable to find.

1

ANNETTE ASKS FOR CELLO LESSONS

"**M**ommy, I want a cello."

"No, Annette, you have to wait until you're five."

"But Mommy, I want a cello."

"You're too young. You have to wait until you're five."

Did we have this conversation every day? Probably not, but she was persistent. She began asking at the age of two, and six months later I gave in. I had discovered her in the living room with a tinkertoy stick in one hand and a large, oblong block in the other. She had appropriated my practice chair for the occasion, and, had she been able to remove it from the case, would probably have been using my cello as well. Announcing her selections, she sang each song while making the proper motions for playing. There sat my tousled strawberry blonde child, so small for her age, so large in her aspirations. I thought, not for the first time, *maybe she really does need a cello.*

I was a part-time professional cellist, and had been performing and teaching for more than twenty years. My current musical life consisted of practicing an hour per day, teaching eight students each week, and serving in a salaried position as Principal Cellist for our local community orchestra, the (Casper) Wyoming Symphony. Just a few years earlier I had completed seven years of teaching at the University of Wisconsin Oshkosh. During the first four years I had taught both university and Suzuki students. Then during the final three I'd taught Suzuki only.

From my Suzuki experience I knew how to locate a one-tenth size cello, the proper sized instrument for a two-year-old. I couldn't pretend that teaching anyone who was that small was as easy as finding an instrument to match. I knew I was taking on a gargantuan task, and so it proved to be.

No matter how much Annette wanted to play the cello, she was still a two-year-old. This made every practice session a challenge: I had to teach a tiny person how to play the cello, and interact with my toddler at the same time. It was exhausting.

But midway through the first year, we hit our stride. I had begun to teach her the basics of rhythmic reading. For this I used a set of flashcards printed with various types of notes and rests, one per card. They could be used in any number or combination. From the very beginning, Annette latched on to this as something exciting. At first I chose all the cards and arranged them as I thought best. But soon she wanted to get in on the fun, and insisted on doing it herself. This played havoc with my set ideas about the order in which certain concepts should be introduced:

"Okay Annette, it's time to do these quarter note flashcards."

"No, Mommy, I want to do *these.*"

And invariably she would pull out the most complicated bunch I had.

At the time, I did not realize that I was up against one of the fundamental realities of dealing with the gifted: their overpowering need to learn things according to their own inner drives, even if this does not match the teacher's plans.

I was a slow learner. My past teaching experience was in part a hindrance, because a pedagogy based on progressive, sequential concepts had for some years served me well. But I had never taught anyone like Annette.

By the time she was 3½ we were spending up to forty-five minutes a day with the cello alone, then following that with as many sets of rhythm flashcards as *I* had the energy for.

"Okay Annette, it's time to stop practicing."

"Please, Mommy, let's do just one more blue la." (The flashcards were blue and we performed them on the syllable "la.")

"All right . . ."

"And *I* get to choose it!"

I also let her arrange the cards, which took a long time. Some days we did as many as five "blue las" before she was ready to stop. Much of the time we did less, and then I was haunted by the knowledge that she could have soaked up two or three times as much learning as I was able to offer her that day. Eventually, her phenomenal attention span convinced me that I was dealing with something entirely new, and that my husband, Ellis, and I had better adapt to it. Thus, although I had no idea how to do it without having first laid the groundwork, I began to try to teach her the difficult concepts she wanted to learn.

Since she loved the blue la flashcards, this activity seemed the logical starting point. The only problem was that when I finally gave her free rein, she would set up five or six lines of something that looked like this:

Then she expected me to teach her how to sing it.

My preference was to begin with something much different:

Not surprisingly, what looks neat, orderly, and predictable on a page of music is often easier to perform than something that looks irregular and cluttered. It is also easier to teach. When confronted with Annette's blue la choices, I'd grope around, then simply jump in:

"Okay, this first note—it's called a whole note. It equals four of these." Here I'd point to the neighboring quarter note flashcard.

"What does 'equals' mean, Mommy?"

Oh no, I'd think. *I wouldn't be having to explain "equals" at this stage if we were working on my blue la.* "Uh, 'equals' means 'exactly the same as.' For example, here are two quarter notes—do you see that they look exactly alike?"

"Yes."

"Well, they sound exactly alike, and four of them fit into a whole note. So, if you were going to sing your blue la, you'd start by deciding how fast your beat is going to be, and what kind of note it should equal."

"I know—let's have the beat equal this!" With great excitement—and apparently at random—she picked up a flashcard with a whole note on it.

"Well, uh . . . but if we do that, it will be almost impossible to sing this blue la. I'm not even sure that *I* could sing it."

"Please try, Mommy. I want to hear what it should sound like."

At this stage I began wondering why I had let the conversation go on so long. I thought, *What teacher in her right mind would do any of this? Annette needs to be singing quarter notes and quarter rests.* I said, "How about we stop this blue la and do a different one—one that I set up?"

"But Mommy, I want to do this one!"

I was unable to see that she actually needed the complexity of the blue la that she had set up. It wasn't that she, or I, should be able to sing it that day, or even anytime soon. She just wanted to direct her own learning, and she knew what she needed.

I did not understand this force in Annette that I was up against; I only realized, vaguely, that to push my simple blue las on her was somehow a mistake. Thus, I floundered on, feeling incompetent, and justifiably so. I had never given a student as much freedom of choice as I gave Annette, and I had no idea what the outcome would be.

My lack of preparation didn't bother her at all. She gobbled every scrap of musical information I could feed her as fast as I could serve it up. While I accepted the necessity of introducing ideas in what I thought was the wrong order, I did not like it. It felt scattered, unsystematic, and disorganized. It seemed as though I was flying by the seat of my pants all the time, as if I could hardly think fast enough to teach her well. In the back of my mind I knew that an excess of organization could be stifling and that creativity was quite messy at certain stages. But I had definite teaching ideas, and was not comfortable with improvisation, either in teaching or playing. However, I learned.

I began to ask Ellis, "Is this normal, this curiosity about assorted scraps of information and concepts that are way too advanced?"

He shrugged, and replied, "It's normal for her."

"Was it normal for you as a child?"

"Yes."

"Is it still how you learn things?"

"Often, yes."

I knew Ellis was unusually bright. I was amazed at his proficiency in math and science, and was equally impressed by my inability to understand most of what he said about it. When a new idea excited him, he'd launch into an explanation, then my brain would begin to fog over and I'd start nodding and trying to look intelligent. At this point he always noticed the glazed look in my eye. We'd continue the conversation for a few more minutes, but then I always gave up.

Before Annette was born, we rarely talked about Ellis' learning processes or his early school experiences. However, as I became more puzzled by her urges to pounce on the most complex musical information available, I began to ask Ellis more questions about his own mind.

My curiosity intensified after our second child, Lewis, was born. Ellis, while watching eighteen-month-old Lewis turn a puzzle upside down and still assemble it effortlessly, would comment, "Yup, it's easy; just turn the picture of the puzzle around in your head." He talked as though his brain was Lewis' brain; there appeared to be no obstacles in his understanding of Lewis' mental processes.

By the time Lewis was two or three years old, I'd had time to get used to the uncanny similarities of intellect between Ellis and the children. However, the first time we discussed Annette and her thirst for complexity, such a close resemblance was a new idea to me. As I quizzed him about the way in which his highly unusual learning processes matched hers, I began to realize that whatever I was up against in teaching Annette, it was a trait shared by at least one other member of our family. Precisely what this trait was, I did not know. The concept, "gifted," was in my mind, but had not yet penetrated my consciousness as a major force in my own life. Talking with Ellis and comparing his learning habits with Annette's, and realizing anew how phenomenally bright they both were, provided my first clue that we might all be in this together. Thus my fog of ignorance about giftedness was pierced by the light of experience: a little stab here, a little one there.

Having taught young children, I did not find Annette's actual cello playing so amazing at first. The physical tasks were about as hard for her as they had been for some of my better three-year-old students from the past, so it was easy to rationalize the amazing things she began to do on the cello. That is, it was easy at first. But soon my credulity was stretched thinner and thinner as I witnessed the unfolding of what appeared to be a picture of the fingerboard and its notes inside her head.

This ability to visualize the fingerboard had come upon me at the age of twenty-four, after I had been playing the cello for sixteen years. It was a concept that I struggled to get across to my other students. It required a thorough understanding of the relationship among three elements: the printed page, the translation of that musical notation into sound, and fingerboard geography. A command of fingerboard geography is not simply the ability to play a given note on any one string, but also to find that same pitch in a different place on another string.

One day Annette said, "Mommy, look at this—I can play these three notes [then she played them] here . . . and then play them again over here [she played them correctly on another spot on a different string], and they sound the same! Isn't that interesting?"

The first time she did this, I thought, *This is normal for a well-taught Suzuki student.* Then a month later, when she did it again with different notes I told myself, *Well, this could be normal.* The next day, after she kept on doing it, my reaction was, *It's possible for a bright, well taught child who has had so much individual attention from a qualified teacher . . .* But finally I was forced to conclude: *This isn't normal . . . This is impossible!*

But possible it was. I could deny it no longer. Her mind was phenomenal. One day she sang a snatch of music for me, then proceeded to announce the correct rhythmic notation: "Mommy, that's a half note, two quarter notes, a quarter rest, and three more quarter notes." I called my sister and told her.

Her response: "You have a prodigy on your hands!"

But I could not bring myself to use that word yet. There seemed so much evidence against it, if you can call your own delusions "evidence." But what were my delusions? Some of them came out of my past teaching experience, both in the classroom and in the private studio. I was systematic and thorough, and excelled at breaking complicated tasks down to their basic components.

While at the University of Wisconsin, I taught Music Theory for the General Student, an introductory course for non-music majors. No previous knowledge of the subject was required. In order to make the course material accessible, I had to think through every step of my own understanding of music theory. I enjoyed this process, and my students did well.

This habit of carefully examining each segment of what I was teaching carried over into the applied (private) cello lessons that were the bulk of my teaching load. A direct result of this refinement in my approach was that my students began sailing through tasks that would have previously caused them trouble. Because of this, they progressed faster, and I came to regard many musical learning problems as surmountable by almost anyone. In fact, this became the driving force behind both my teaching and my own practicing. So when Annette's total musical comprehension began to grow by giant leaps after only a year of daily lessons with me, I still wasn't too surprised. That is, I tried not to be.

I told myself, *she's been hearing me play the cello since she was conceived. That's why it's starting to come so easily . . . She's picking it up so fast because I work with her every day.* Basic music theory and reading aren't all that difficult, I had discovered. My college students had no trouble with it. My high school students had no trouble with it. Even my junior high students could get it without a lot of effort. But with Annette I had a strange case of amnesia: I conveniently forgot that she was only three years old.

My denials about her brilliance were not limited to the connection I tried to draw between my teaching methods and her rapid progress. I also applied the diet-and-environment rationale. Ellis and I had developed eating habits which differed radically from the norm: we prepared everything from scratch, rarely ate in restaurants, never consumed fast food or convenience food, drank filtered water, and bought as many organic products as we could afford. We were not surprised that our children were alert and clear-headed. Plus, we constantly stimulated their minds in one way or another.

One day I complained to Ellis that I hadn't read even one book in the entire year since Lewis was born. He replied, "Yes you have. You've read *Goodnight Moon, The Cat in the Hat, The Runaway Bunny, Mother Goose . . .*" It did seem like I had spent the whole first year of Lewis' life sitting on the couch nursing him and reading to Annette (in my sleep). I was at home with our children except during minimal teaching and symphony rehearsal hours. We knew we were providing a rich environment, so Annette's and Lewis' high intelligence seemed a logical outgrowth of that rather than something extraordinary.

My relative ignorance about musical prodigies, especially their early lives, was another factor in my continuing self-deception. Did Rostropovich have major problems with his bow hold during his first year of cello playing? And children who dazzled international audiences at the age of . . . well, what age? Anywhere from seven to twelve? What were their beginnings? I wasn't sure. I read *My Son, Yo-Yo,* a book by Yo-Yo Ma's mother about his early life, but it lacked many of the details of the cello that I was seeking. When did he begin vibrato?[1] Did it spring up in full bloom on the first try? Did he have trouble learning to keep his bow in contact with the string? Was his left hand position perfect from the day he picked up the cello? Such information would have been immensely helpful, but all I had were my day-to-day observations of Annette. I did not want to call up current or former colleagues and say, "I think my daughter might be a musical prodigy. How do I tell?"

I also knew that there was a difference between an actual prodigy and a very good player who happened to be young. The Suzuki movement had produced many good young players. Their early abilities appeared to stem directly from a systematic pedagogy which was aimed at helping young children become the best musicians they could be.

Musical prodigies are part of a much longer history and, for all I knew, sprang out of nowhere and flourished no matter what their early environment. Since Annette had undeniable early advantages similar to those provided by Suzuki instruction, I could easily talk myself out of the idea that she was a prodigy. My stereotypes also included the idea that a prodigy would be performing brilliantly, in public, by the age of five or six. Annette, while progressing faster than anyone I had ever taught, did not seem to be headed

---

[1] The oscillating motion in the left hand which helps to give a vocal quality to the string player's sound.

in precisely that direction. This bolstered my denials about the extent of her abilities.

My pedagogical development at the time I began teaching Annette was yet another pillar for my denials. I had evolved a number of wildly unconventional ideas about cello playing. My practicing had been my lab, and my students willing guinea pigs. Nowhere did the extremity of my approach show more clearly than in the teaching of beginners. My way of starting cellists appeared to hinder their progress and make their early efforts unduly complex. For example, I spent inordinate amounts of time on keeping the fingers of the left hand[2] close together. This made more advanced skills, especially shifting and vibrato, easier in the long run, but it complicated the way in which the fingers moved between adjacent notes. With the hand bunched up, a slide (shift) was necessary for every note change. This made the simplest pieces difficult.

As I watched Annette working to master *Twinkle, Twinkle, Little Star* and other beginning pieces, it did not surprise me that her efforts were mostly unspectacular. She was working on many things all at once: shifting, listening for pitch, left hand position and fluency, and future vibrato. I knew it would all pay off, but meanwhile it was easy to imagine that her learning curve would remain gentle and gradual, thus excusing her from the hazards of being a prodigy and me from believing that she was one.

I could cling to this denial because I relied on myth, not fact, and could design my self-deceptions in whatever way I chose. Yet no matter how I rationalized the progress of her cello technique, I could

---

[2] The left hand traverses the fingerboard; the right hand holds the bow.

not mistake the brilliance of her mind. Music theory continued to be easy for her. At the age of four she could do elementary sight singing and rhythmic dictation.[3] Before the age of five, she composed a six-bar musical theme. Her memory was unbelievable. I couldn't ignore these things, and didn't try to. Rather, I worked progressively harder to explain them on some other basis than that of her being a genius. I kept that word at bay for a long time; it would flicker in my thoughts and I would stomp it out.

---

[3] Sight singing is to sing a musical passage from the printed page without first having heard it. Rhythmic dictation is to write down the correct rhythmic notation (e.g. quarter notes, eighth notes, etc.) for a passage that has been performed for you but which you have not seen on the printed page.

2

ANNETTE LEARNS TO READ

The development of Annette's verbal and reading ability was another clue to her giftedness. By the age of eighteen months she had a vocabulary of more than 300 words, and by twenty months she knew all the letters of the alphabet. This was one of the first things that sent me to the library in search of more information. It was the beginning of my discovery that giftedness is not a popular subject. The handful of books I found left many of my questions unanswered and served mainly to whet my appetite for more. Was there a difference between "gifted" and "merely bright?" If so, how could I tell? I had read Tasha Tudor's beautiful book, *A is for Annabelle,* to Annette dozens of times. Of course she had it practically memorized—who wouldn't? She seemed to thrive on repetition and learning, but I figured that was normal. As for vocabulary, I was a talkative person, plus Ellis and I read to her constantly. She had been surrounded by words all her life—of course she was a talker.

While reading to her I loved to cuddle her on my lap and put my cheek against her soft, wispy hair. I was dreaming of the baby to come, Lewis, who was already shrinking my lap.

That was fine with Annette. When I wasn't reading to her, she was off on her own business around the house. She had lost the desire to cuddle at about one year of age. I'd reach for her and she'd say, "No!" and back hastily away, a stubborn look in her blue eyes.

Stubborn or businesslike, those were the two expressions I saw crossing her face more often than any others at that age. The businesslike set of her whole being was most evident when I let her shut the clasps on my cello case. She'd give each clasp her complete attention as I watched her profile: the turned-up nose that was a fortunate blend of Ellis' ski jump and my straight slide.

Many things changed with the birth of Lewis. He was hungry and persistently awake, even as an infant—so much so that he seemed to actively resist sleep. Ellis and I were busy and exhausted. Annette was more often left to her own resources, and her imagination and speaking vocabulary began to grow in tandem. She wove long, complicated tales about her stuffed animals and their adventures. When she wasn't doing that, she was usually lying on her bed, wide awake, sucking her thumb and thinking. At such times she was perfectly content. This struck me as quite unusual for a two-year-old, but I didn't have much time to ponder it.

After lavishing so much attention on her when she had been an only child, I worried that we were neglecting her. True, I read to her throughout that first year of breastfeeding Lewis, but as he got more active, I got busier and even more tired. For about six months, Annette hovered on the edge of learning to read:

"Does 'Daddy' start with an A?"

"No, Annette. If 'Daddy' started with an A, it would be 'Addy!'" Then she would giggle, as we launched into what I called "goofy phonics":

"Annette, if 'Daddy' started with an M, what would it be?"

Pause . . . "Maddy!"

"How about an S?"

"Saddy!"

"How about a T?"

"Taddy!"

As with cello practicing, her appetite for this was insatiable. I was painfully aware that she was more than ready to learn to read, but I did not have time to teach her. Ellis and I were already spreading ourselves far thinner than was good for us.

In theory Ellis' schedule was flexible because he had his own home remodeling business. If he absolutely had to, he could work on a Saturday morning instead of a Thursday afternoon. Before we faced the problem of how I was going to fit in reading lessons, we had struggled with scheduling Annette's cello practicing. How was I going to give my full attention to teaching her—and protect an expensive musical instrument—while chasing one-year-old Lewis all over the house?

I tried teaching her after supper when Ellis was home, but we soon realized that it was the wrong time of day for her; she was too tired. We concluded that Annette needed to practice in the morning right after breakfast. So Ellis adjusted his schedule to stay home and take care of Lewis during Annette's practice time. Because of this, his workday sometimes began two hours late, or more, depending on when I could pry myself away from Annette's curiosity. This change in Ellis' work schedule was the first in a series of major financial and time sacrifices that we made in order to teach our children at home.

As Annette's imaginative tales became longer and more intricate, it seemed to me that she was starving for some kind of creative outlet. Finally, in September of 1996, when she was 3½, and Lewis 1½, I began giving her reading lessons. By a miracle, Lewis was willing to sit on the couch with us while Annette and I read.

We used the McGuffey's Eclectic Reader series, starting with the Primer. Since she knew most of her consonants, she needed little help. All I had to do was tell her whether the vowels were long or short, then encourage her to sound out the words. For about two months she was content to do just one page per day, plus a complete review of previous lessons. Then she started asking to work ahead. I tried to overrule this, but she insisted. So one morning we skipped four or five lessons, and she had a great time trying to read a bunch of difficult new words. I was still attached to my systematic teaching style, so it was difficult for me to let her do this, but I had to. She so obviously needed it. Just one day of acceleration seemed to satisfy her, but a few weeks later, this same push to skip forward reasserted itself.

I kept saying, "But Annette, it's too hard. You'll get confused."

This idea did not trouble her. She was exhibiting precisely the same learning trait—a thirst for complexity—that I had encountered in her musical studies. Why didn't I see it? I remember thinking, *What will I do if she comes to long words that have too many new phonics all at once? How will I ever untangle it for her?*

Here was my convenient amnesia again. Although I had just witnessed the way in which she "coped" with "difficulties," that incident in which we skipped four or five lessons must have occupied a separate, sealed compartment in my consciousness. Did this sealed chamber bear a sign marked, "I can't account for this, therefore I won't consider it?" I don't know.

However, I do remember that I had myself convinced that I was worried about confusing her when I was actually anxious about having to adapt to a new teaching situation. Only her stubborn insistence changed me, and it didn't change my thinking. Instead, it broke down my determination; I had to let her skip forward because she wore me down.

One day she did four new lessons (after reviewing thirty-one), and didn't want to stop. About ten days later, she finished the Primer and asked for the First Reader. I just handed it to her. As with the cello, her attention span had quickly overtaken my available teaching time.

We worked together on the First Reader at the rate of two to fifteen new lessons per day. She finished it in a month. In mid-January, shortly before the age of four, Annette began the Second Reader. This book has seventy-one lessons and 160 paperback sized pages, and she completed it in late May. Here is a sample sentence from one of the later lessons: "So, day after day, Davy hunted the woods for the prettiest flowers, and the most dainty ferns and mosses." (McGuffey 1920, 147)

I had no idea what grade level this was. When I finally consulted a friend of ours who taught elementary school, she answered, "somewhere above second grade." This did not shock me as it should have because I was ignorant about the formula for determining someone's IQ. I knew nothing about the subject except, vaguely, that "somewhere around 140 or above" was "genius level." The only other thing I knew was that not one of my brighter cello students— and I had some who were intellectually brilliant— knew his or her IQ. I now believe this to be a scandal. How have we gone so wrong as a society that basic information about a national resource, our most brilliant young people, is so utterly absent?

My attitude didn't help. Though I was amazed and thrilled at Annette's developmental pace, and Lewis' also, my denials about the reality of our situation held. My reading material and thoughts from this time period are illuminating both of my thirst for information and my ignorance and willful blindness. I read a library book by Sheila and Joseph Perino, *Parenting the Gifted: Developing the Promise.* This book described one gifted child who "was able to tell time by her third birthday, and had a basic sight vocabulary in reading by 2½ years." (Perino and Perino 1981, 22)

Annette was then going on five, and could not tell time. She was an early, avid reader, but not at the age of two. Somehow I had it fixed in my mind that really brilliant people learn to read at about two years of age. On this evidence, I concluded that Annette, though bright, was not exceptional.

In the Perinos' book I read about Michael Grost, a prodigy who did not speak a word until the age of eighteen months. Then he spoke in complete sentences. From *Genius in Residence,* his mother's chronicle of his childhood, I learned that Michael had taught himself to read before the age of three (Grost 1970, 27). By five years of age he had read an entire encyclopedia and was having adult level conversations with his mother. I was attracted to Michael's story because he was a late talker. In *Parenting the Gifted,* the authors cited this as an example of how widely the most gifted young children can differ from the norm, and from each other. I wondered if Annette was one of these. But I had constructed an equation in my head: she hadn't done the things that these other highly gifted children had done, at those particular ages; therefore she was bright, but not exceptional.

She continued to do amazing things in her cello studies. And she began reading more and more books. We had to pry her loose from Childcraft volumes, Laura Ingalls Wilder books, and the original Dr. Dolittle series. Her vocabulary and comprehension grew exponentially. Every time she did something brilliant, I thought, *Is she a genius?* My rather lame answer to myself was, *No, of course not . . . How could she be a genius?* Why did I cling to this position? Another lame excuse: *Well, nobody is a genius. Not an actual genius. Well, some people are, but not in my family! How could it happen in my family?*

How could I think, *Nobody is a genius?* Who was Albert Einstein, if not one of the most brilliant people of all time? I knew there was a phenomenon in the world called genius. I couldn't ignore that. But I could, and did, fix my mind on the image of an adult genius, and gave it a label: "famous."

From that I concluded that nobody in my family would ever be famous, therefore, Annette wasn't a genius. I did not stop to ask myself what Einstein was like when he was three years old. It was far easier to reserve my curiosity about prodigious early development for those few unsatisfactory books. I could thus compartmentalize my thinking. That way, when confronted with Annette's brilliant feats, I could continue to tell myself, Yes, she's certainly bright, but not a genius.

I also noticed that I was talking about our children less and less. When asked, "What are Annette and Lewis doing now?" I answered, "Oh, you know, the usual things." People didn't press for details, so I didn't have to tell them that Annette knew more about the natural world than I did, and that Lewis, before the age of two, had memorized a fifty-one piece puzzle which he could assemble in ten minutes. Family and friends knew about these things, but as time passed I also shared less detail with many of them. I did this in self-defense. I did not want to expose myself to the barrage of disbelief, bad advice, criticism, and other nonsense parents of exceptional children bring upon themselves when they merely tell the truth about what is going on in their homes. I'd had a little, but enough, experience with this, and all of the books told me that now I could expect more of it.

The books were unanimous on one other point: a fight was ahead if we expected the public schools to properly educate our children. Whole chapters were devoted to the forming of parent groups, lobbying the school board, plus incurring the time and expense of proving your child's giftedness to doubting administrators. It sounded like a tremendous amount of work and emotional stress. I began to realize that we could put the same amount of time and energy into home schooling, with far happier results. Thus, about two years before Annette reached kindergarten age, we made our final decision to home school our children.

We didn't know much about the schools in our community, and weren't motivated to investigate. I had read of nationwide declines in standards and test scores, the rise of athletics over academics, and sex education for first graders. It seemed reasonable to suppose that our local school district had been at least partially infected with these ills. I had graduated from high school in Casper twenty years ago, and at that time the core curriculum had already begun to deteriorate. I also found more direct evidence that our local district was not set up for gifted students. In our occasional encounters with local elementary school teachers, their comments, if they heard Annette read, were always the same: "There's no classroom in this city that could provide what she needs!"

When I turned my back on the public schools, I also rejected any thought of intelligence testing for Annette and Lewis. The books always mentioned it in the context of forcing the schools to do right by gifted children in the face of incontrovertible proof. Much less often did I read that IQ testing could be helpful to parents for any number of other reasons. For example, I had no idea it could be helpful to me either personally or in my role as the major teacher of my children.

Once again, my ignorance was at work. I knew nothing about IQ tests; the only information I had came from my assumptions, mostly wrong. I did not view IQ tests as a tool for understanding intelligence. I didn't really know what they were for. I had never been given one, although I had often wondered about my own IQ. IQ testing was a vague, fuzzy area in my mind relegated to the same category as Mensa, which I then equated with snobbery. Whenever I thought about "IQ," especially "high IQ," I saw instant pictures of people like Ellis, who could solve complicated visual and mathematical puzzles.

In all of these ways my attitudes reflected societal stereotypes about high intelligence: those who have it, what it is, and how to measure it. This ignorance was not helpful to me, Ellis, or our children. However, I did not know that Annette and Lewis, in combination with my own curiosity, were all steering me toward a fault line inside myself under which lay a major earthquake waiting to happen.

3

OUR CHILDREN ARE NOT NORMAL

At the dawn of Annette's existence, a few things happened which I classified as flukes because they were so improbable.

The first incident occurred sometime before she was eight weeks old. About six evenings a month I had to attend symphony rehearsals; and although we had a new baby, we figured we could manage it. However, Annette would not take a bottle, and needed to nurse almost continuously from before supper time until bedtime. This happened evening after evening no matter how much I nursed her during the day. Rehearsal nights became a miserable experience for everyone, Annette and Ellis most of all. One evening, however, I returned home to find her patiently waiting on Ellis' lap.

This was his tale: as usual, she had screamed her way through the first few hours of my absence. All his attempts to quiet her had failed, and it began to be more than he could take. Finally, in desperation, he held her up to his face and said, "Annette! You have GOT to stop fussing!!" She was quiet from that moment on. Ellis makes no claim that she understood the words, only that he got through.

Annette was between five and six months old when she did in fact understand something I said to her. She had a rattle that was big and heavy relative to her size. When lying on her back and holding it, she couldn't just wave her arm and get it to make noise: concerted effort was necessary. I was kneeling over her, encouraging her to shake it back and forth. She stared with interest at me, but did nothing. Finally I said, "Annette, flop your arm!" and touched the hand that held the rattle. She flopped, and the rattle rattled. During the entire incident I had deliberately not made the correct motion with my arm. That is how I know that she understood my words—she had no other clues.

I ran to the phone and called my sister. Her response to my story was, "Oh, you're just a doting mom. You must have moved your arm and she imitated it." Of course I was a doting mom, but that didn't change the other facts. I did alter my interpretation, however, and decided that I had witnessed another fluke. After all, how could she have understood my actual words? She was only 5½ months old.

Last, but not least, she read a word—one word—off her crib railing. She was between twenty and twenty-three months old. The word was "side": she looked at it, pointed to it, and said it. Then she looked up at us. Incredulous, I searched her face, as I had so often done when she was an infant. What was going on inside that fuzzy little head? She had just given me a gigantic clue, but I ignored it.

I argued with Ellis about this incident for months.

How could it have been reading? She wasn't reading any other words except "Mom," off one of my maternity sweatshirts. In my opinion, reading included comprehension, and a functional vocabulary. I maintained that only two words did not constitute reading. Ellis' answer was: "You were there. What did she do?" My rather feeble response was, "She said 'side' but it wasn't reading! It couldn't have been reading. Besides, she hasn't done it again." True, she only did it once, but that did not change the facts: she looked at the word, pointed to it, and said it. I recalled this episode four years later, shortly after her IQ test, and thought, *How else would the life of a genius begin, but with events such as this? Why didn't I see it for what it was at the time?* The answer is that I didn't see it because I wouldn't: my attitudes were too entrenched. Other people were more than ready to tell me that I was imagining things, and I was a willing party to this whole process of denial.

Ellis was an excellent foil to these negative influences within and outside of me. He had a long history of seeing the truth and telling it. Where I wanted to interpret and deny things that the children did, he asked simple questions such as, "What did you see? What did he do?"

If I argued, as I had after the "side" incident, he always responded with more basic questions: "What happened? What are the facts?" By observing and listening to the children without interpretation or misjudgment he led the way for me, and also gave Annette and Lewis the greatest gift a parent can give to a child: understanding. I knew that his approach was better than mine, but my denials were strong, and still they held.

Certainly a few months after the "side" incident

and a few weeks into Lewis' life, I could lay a more legitimate claim to being out of touch with reality. I lived in a fog of chronic sleep deprivation. I will never forget the first night that he refused to go to sleep— he wasn't even a month old. I had some prior success nursing him to sleep most nights by midnight, then snatching an hour or two of rest before the next feeding. But that night, he didn't close his eyes at all. I had been nursing him for what seemed like hours, and had dozed off. Then I awoke thinking, *He's quiet! Thank God he's finally asleep!* I looked down, and his eyes were wide open. They were enormous, alive, and blue. They stared out of his chubby pink face as if to devour the whole world without wasting an instant. I was barely recovered from his birth, and in dire need of rest. When I found myself looking straight into his eyes, I thought I would lose my mind right then and there, in our living room at 2:30 in the morning, February 2, 1995.

This was the first of many such episodes. I was not of the "let them cry" school of baby care, and figured that if the baby was fussing, he or she needed something. Many were the nights that we checked and re-checked the diaper. It was usually dry, because it had just been changed. The diaper pins were never open. I nursed Lewis for hours every evening, especially around bedtime. Then Ellis would walk him around for ten or fifteen minutes and put him in his crib. Then we would try to go to sleep. It was a joke. We lay there and listened to him howl for a while, then the inevitable conversation began:

"Did you check the diaper?"

"Yes, did you get a burp?"

"Yes, do you suppose he's sick?"

"I don't know. He's not hot."

"Shall I go walk with him?"

"Aren't you tired?"

"Yes, aren't you?"

"Well, we both have a lot to do tomorrow . . ."

"Is Annette asleep?"

"I think so, but she won't be tomorrow when Lewis is."

"What are we going to do? Why is he still crying? Why does he do this every night?"

"I'll go walk with him."

By the time Lewis had his two-month checkup, we'd become so sleep-deprived that life was almost unlivable. We were desperate, and decided that we'd better start experimenting. According to the doctor—and our own instincts—Lewis was perfectly healthy, therefore we felt that perhaps he could weather a few mistakes.

We began with the understanding that Lewis was unhappy about something, and whatever that something was, it wasn't changing very fast, if at all. He seemed to have a grievance against sleep itself. It soon became obvious to us that this was the main problem. He was already starting to fight against his morning and afternoon naps. He always lost, but sometimes it was a bitter struggle. He was dogged in this resistance to sleep. We finally realized that he wanted to stay awake all the time because he was so interested in his environment. But what normal, healthy baby isn't? In what way was Lewis so unusual? Simply that he was excessively absorbed in his surroundings. He didn't want to miss anything—not one second—and sleep was a thief that stole from him precious hours of learning and observation. It was one of Lewis' earliest lessons about the realities of life. He needed rest, and also had to learn to conform to the family's sleep schedule.

We did not arrive at all of these conclusions simultaneously. We merely began by observing him, trusting our instincts, and letting him cry for longer periods at bedtime. Something *was* wrong, but there was no short-term solution. The answer to the problem was for Lewis to get older, to need less sleep, and to become more of a participant in his world. In short, he needed to stop being a baby and start being a toddler. He eventually adjusted to the idea that he was stuck in his crib at bedtime, and had better make the best of it. Gradually we were able to achieve a minimum level of regular sleep, but it only happened because we were willing to change our tactics.

I knew from my reading that unusual alertness in infancy was one of the signs of giftedness. I didn't doubt it, because of the many other traits which Lewis displayed before the age of one year, and because I was beginning to get used to the idea of having gifted children. I still hadn't learned not to talk about it, but my ability to handle these conversations improved:

Family Friend: And how are your children doing?

Me: Oh, fine. I just wish Lewis would sleep a little more.

FF: Yes, I know what you mean, especially with another child to take care of.

Me: Well, for all I know it could be a blessing. Supposedly, if a child is an alert infant, that could be an indicator of high intelligence.

FF: Where did you learn this?

Me: In a book about giftedness that I checked

out of the library. I keep borrowing the same book because it has a long list of developmental milestones. I am trying to figure out just how bright Annette is, and I keep forgetting what's on the list.

FF: You just can't help yourself, can you? (General laughter, in which I join)

It was true that I could not help myself. Denial was losing out to my insatiable hunger for information. I needed to know just how bright our children were, and I was still grossly ignorant about the whole subject.

Lewis did a lot to convince us that he was not normal and never would be. At the age of three months he laughed out loud at the sight of Annette and Ellis being silly together on the living room floor. That, I knew, was phenomenally early. Then there was the day he spent at least an hour entertaining himself by scooting around with a washcloth—throwing it, chewing it, bunching it up, and generally having a high old time. I kept waiting for him to get bored, but he got hungry first. He was then about nine months old, not crawling, not rolling over. He sat, and he scooted. At his six-month checkup, I had truthfully told the doctor that he had rolled over. He had done so, once. But never again: he preferred to lie on his back, and later on, to sit, in order to look, listen, and absorb with all his being. He was too busy to bother with rolling over.

I had been determined to delay solid food until he was six months old. But at five months, he insisted. He wanted to sit at the table like the rest of us. With the advent of baby cereal, I expected the weeks of entertainment and messes that we had experienced with Annette. Not so: on the second bite, he figured out how to get it to the back of his mouth and swallow it. I was shocked, of course. With shock came a feeble resurgence of denial: *Well, he's a boy, and boys seem to be more serious about eating than girls are . . . That's why he caught on right away.* But it was nonsense. Physical tasks gave him little or no trouble. Once he had tried to do something a few times, he could do it. The second day he was in the high chair, I stuck a bottle in his face. He had taken many a bottle in the previous months, but that day he just looked at me like I was crazy. He wanted a cup. So I gave him one, with a spout, and he mastered it. My sister's comment was, "He's quite a perceptive little person. He noticed that everyone else had a cup, and he wanted one too." I don't know if she was aware that this remark signaled the beginning of her slippery slide into doting aunthood.

At that time we had alphabet letters with magnets on the back. Annette enjoyed these a lot, especially after she figured out how to get them to stick to the refrigerator. She made many attempts over a period of months before she finally figured out which side of the letter had to face the refrigerator. Not so with Lewis: the first day I sat down with him to play with the letters, he quickly figured out, by himself, how to make them stick. He didn't forget. He was eleven months old. Later I told Ellis, "He figured it out on the second or third try! He must be even brighter than Annette." Ellis answered, "Not necessarily brighter, just different."

The concept "equally bright but different" had finally begun to penetrate my consciousness. Before Lewis was one year old he was already more interested in numbers than Annette was at the age of almost three. Consequently, his facility with them, fed by what seemed pure enjoyment of math, put him far ahead of where Annette had been at the same age. The way in which his memory worked also differed from Annette's. Where she had unlimited capacity for, and delight in, repetition, Lewis preferred to store things at the first or second hearing, then move on. Annette preferred books; Lewis liked magnets and blocks.

One day while watching Lewis, Ellis commented, "He has a mechanical mind." True, he was fascinated with shape sorters, puzzles, and anything that he could build with. He had a love affair with Legos: I would pass through the kitchen and find him happily constructing what looked like a hodgepodge to me. But the way in which he sorted through the pile of loose blocks, the care with which he selected the perfect one, the delicate precision with which he installed it in just the right place, all spoke to me of a love for invention, design, and assembly. I saw these subtleties: the love, care, and exactness that he brought to all of his building projects. I noted it to myself as a probable sign of brilliance.

This was something I knew better than to breathe a word of to anyone but Ellis. After all, whose child does not play with blocks? What remark could better elicit a hoot of derision from just about anyone than, "My son loves to build complicated structures with his Legos and Tinkertoys. I can see his enthrallment in the very way that he handles each piece. I think this is a sign of high intelligence."

I would get this far in my imaginary conversation with an acquaintance or family member before I got interrupted with a snicker and a remark such as, "Right, your kid is a genius. Every parent thinks his child is brilliant. Get real!"

I never imagined myself being articulate enough to add that he was less than one year old at the time that he sat for forty-five minutes to an hour a day working on his building projects. Around this time, I did have an actual conversation with one of my colleagues who was also a cellist. Her children were only a few years older than mine. We were comparing their ages, and she commented, "I know how busy you are with your children right now. Before the age of eighteen months they're just not capable of entertaining themselves."

Automatically I nodded, then gulped as pictures shot through my head, images of nine-month-old Lewis scooting around playing with the washcloth, eleven-month-old Lewis riveted to his blocks. It wasn't just the length of time that he concentrated; as with Annette and her thumb-sucking, he was perfectly quiet and content. I could see inside his mind on these occasions and could tell that he was at the pinnacle of living as he then knew it.

One day I watched him select the round shape sorter piece, find the round hole, and put it in. He did this correctly ten times in a row. I rushed right over and gave him one of the other shapes, but he wasn't interested. He liked the round one. For months, that was all he did with the shape sorter. There it was again: the love of precision, the deep satisfaction in fitting the right shape into the right place. When Ellis started making wooden puzzles, we saw it again. He would find the right piece, fit it with another one, remove it, then put it back. Nothing else existed for Lewis on these occasions except the glory of putting pieces together, pulling them apart, putting them together, and pulling them apart.

He was so absorbed that I realized that Ellis could probably leave him and go off to work while I practiced with Annette. We decided to try it. After breakfast, dishes, diapers, and other chores, the three of us would settle down: Annette and I with the cello in the living room, and Lewis with his fifty-one piece wooden puzzle in the kitchen. He would dump it out and go after it like he hadn't seen it in weeks. He was so quiet that I was compelled to check on him frequently until I realized that he was locked in. I began to see that these daily opportunities for solitude were quite important to him.

Despite these long, quiet periods of total absorption at such an early age, life with Lewis was far from peaceful. As a tiny baby, he resented being burped. I sat him up on my lap, patted him on the back, and he fussed and pushed back against my hand with all his strength. If I got my way, he cried and cried. If he got his way, which he did occasionally, I got a mess. So I insisted on burping, but to him it was a perpetual grievance, one I heard about at full volume until he could resume nursing. Anytime something upset him, we could tell that the end of his world had come. I was later to learn that this sort of emotional intensity is one of the hallmarks of giftedness.

This depth of feeling had its delightful side: Lewis was returning hugs at eight months of age. He hugged close and hard. He held his stuffed animals the same way. As I watched him I thought, *Some lucky woman is going to get the world's most affectionate husband.* He was surely the most intense person I had ever known: one day not long after that first hug, I had to take something away from him. He cried as though I had cut him, and wrapped his empty arms around himself exactly as he hugged us. He cried

and squeezed, cried and squeezed, over and over
again, like a little bellows. It was not temper, but all-
consuming grief. I almost cried myself, it was so painful to witness. I thought, *What kind of life is this poor
child going to have if he takes everything to heart so absolutely? He'll never survive unless he learns to get over things.*
But I knew what kind of life he would have, because
I was exactly like him. And so far I had survived, but
not by "learning to get over things."

During this time period, Ellis and I had many
conversations about his early childhood. I knew that
he had walked at the age of six months, and I kept
quizzing him about it:

"Six months? Are you sure? How did it happen?"

"Of course I'm sure. Mama wouldn't forget a
thing like that."

"She must have gone crazy, having you mobile at
that age."

"I'm sure it wasn't easy for her."

"And you say Lewis is a lot like you at that age—
he isn't like you in that respect!"

Lewis never did crawl. He went from sitting and
scooting to pulling up. He ended up cruising and
walking at the normal time. A few years later I
learned from my uncle that my mother had also
scooted, and never crawled. I wondered if her mo-
bility had taken the same route as Lewis' for the same
reasons. She had graduated from high school early
and attended college at age sixteen. I knew my family was bright, but I did not know then that giftedness runs in families. If someone had told me so, I
probably would have agreed, but would also have
been quick to point out that it had bypassed me.

I knew that my family's oddness had not bypassed

me. At that time, however, I had no clue that oddness and giftedness go together.

My mother was concerned about the effects of plastic on the environment when few others were. She washed her used plastic bags and took them with her back to the grocery store to put that week's produce in. I am sure she got plenty of stares from her fellow shoppers, because this was in the 1960s when concern for the environment was hardly the American Way. She also began eating (and feeding us) granola, natural peanut butter, and whole wheat bread several decades before other parents of her generation had even thought of it.

Mom also had a violent aversion to television. She would notice other people's TVs flickering in their living rooms at dusk and comment, "There's the blue ghost again." Then she'd add, "When I'm on my deathbed in the hospital, I'm not going to stand for one of those things flickering at me during the last days of my life. I can't imagine anything worse."

I remember my mother at home in the evenings with her feet up, reading thick books. Every corner of our house was crammed with books. My father sold books for a living. He seemed always to be reading, or talking about, Tolstoy and Shakespeare.

All of this was normal for our family, and I thought little of it until, in my late twenties, I had a revealing conversation with a friend of the family.

I told her, "Now that I have a full-time job in music, I have a bit of time in the evenings. I'm also kind of tired, my brain even more than my body, so I've been reading a lot of junk."

She replied, "Okay, tell me what you're reading—I want to know what *your* family considers 'junk'!"

I don't remember what titles I had chosen from the library for easy reading, but it certainly was not junk by her standards. I knew my family was not normal, and I was aware that all of our reading material pointed toward above average intelligence. But somehow I always focused on our shared eccentricities and did not connect the accompanying, and obvious, signs of high intellect with myself.

This same friend had once commented to me, "I'm so impressed with your musical abilities."

I said, "Oh goodness, I'm just an average cellist—probably below average. It's Yo-Yo Ma and others like him that are impressive."

She laughed as if I'd said something absurd, and answered, "Becky, do you have any idea—any clue—what percentage of people who have ever played a musical instrument stay with it and work at it the way you have?"

I hadn't thought about it. I had only noticed, absently, that my roommates in graduate school liked to go out on weekend evenings, whereas I usually spent that time practicing. Then, fifteen years later, I was spending even more time practicing, first with Annette, then with Lewis also.

4

LEWIS ASKS FOR CELLO LESSONS

As Annette's cello lessons progressed, Lewis, age twenty months, began to migrate to the living room to watch us. It was crowded. Our large new couch took up about a quarter of the available space. Annette and I sat on a scrap of carpet which was supposed to protect our hardwood floor from the ravages of cello endpins. I sat with my back to the couch, trying to work with Annette, while Lewis said, "Mommy, please teach me to play the cello." I answered, "No, Lewis, you're too young. You have to wait until you're two and a half."

I thought I had good reasons for not wanting to start Lewis on the cello. I was so busy and tired that I could not imagine cramming in one more thing. And despite my success with Annette, I was fundamentally opposed to the teaching of stringed instruments to very young children. When Annette was a few months old, I remember Ellis asking me about this: "If she shows any interest in music, are you going to teach her the cello?" "Well, maybe," I replied, "but I can tell you one thing, there won't be any of this Suzuki nonsense!"

This remark caught me totally off guard. I was then still advertising myself as a Suzuki teacher, though I had no young students. But after that conversation I began to examine my attitudes and soon realized that teaching three-year-olds to play the cello was something I did not want to do, and no longer believed in.

Dr. Shinichi Suzuki founded his philosophy on the premise that young children can learn to play a musical instrument by a process similar to language acquisition. From birth, children hear their native tongue spoken; from birth, they should listen to music. Parents talk, children imitate them. The same will occur if the parent(s) learn to play a musical instrument. When children are learning to talk they repeat new words over and over again, at the same time using their accumulated vocabulary. Musical proficiency should also be built this way, by continuing to practice old pieces while adding new ones. This contrasts with the time-honored method of mastering a piece, then putting it aside and going on to the next one. Also in direct conflict with tradition is the delay in reading music. Children become fluent talkers before they learn to read; Dr. Suzuki reasoned that they should also become fluent players—or at least establish the basics of technique—before they learn music reading.

I was not the first Suzuki teacher to discover that this created musical illiteracy. A whole pedagogy evolved just to deal with this problem. Children who were too young to easily understand the abstractions of music reading became such skilled players that they did not want to slow down and undergo the rigors of note reading. I helped cause these problems in many of my students and then worked to apply the emerging preventive ideas. But my heart was not in it. I suspected that the Suzuki philosophy was the real problem.

I had other objections to Suzuki pedagogy— probably the strongest was that I could not be true to myself. The repertoire, procedures, and philosophy were clearly defined, and I felt suffocated. I was not fully conscious of this at the time I was struggling to be a good Suzuki teacher. I thought that my main problem was three-year-old students and their parents. I felt like an entertainer, cheerleading squad, and therapist, not a teacher.

When I finally consented to give Annette cello lessons, I was determined to do things differently. We did few of the usual Suzuki activities. I did not require her to listen to tape recordings of her pieces, nor did we make up words to match her bowing rhythms. I did not invent games to help her master skills; we just worked. When her mind wandered I could terminate the practice session. This was not an option when I was paid to teach someone else's child. I had leverage with Annette, because she had asked me for lessons. If she was that motivated, I figured that the length of her practice sessions would be right because it would be dictated by her drive to learn. The more I focused on her interests and desires in lessons, the more we deviated from any tradition or pedagogy that I was aware of. Thus, although I began by leaning on a few of my Suzuki teaching skills, I had to abandon almost everything I thought I knew. This left me in a state of continual experimentation. It was working, but only because she was my own child.

Lewis asked for lessons almost every day. I began to feel his intense longing, his attraction to the cello and to music. He sang often, always in tune. He needed a cello, and couldn't understand why he had to do without one. This drive to become a musician wouldn't leave him alone, and it wouldn't leave me alone either.

As I helped Annette with her practicing and Lewis sat right there watching us every morning, I began to think about Almanzo, in Laura Ingalls Wilder's *Farmer Boy.* The story's central conflict is that Almanzo wants a colt, but his father thinks he's too young. He and the reader both realize that he is not too young. He has the necessary patience and maturity, and most of all the desire. But his father is adamant because of Almanzo's chronological age.

I never thought I would give in before Lewis reached 2½, but I did. His pull toward music was part of the reason, but he also had a consuming drive to become a grown up person. He had noticed that he was the youngest member of the household, and it was a sore point with him. We learned not to speak of him as being "short," and Annette "taller," because to him "short" and "not grown up" were identical. He couldn't stand being so young, so cut off from the activities of the tall world. Once I began to see this, my resistance crumbled fast. I realized that maybe he knew, better than I did, what he actually needed.

Cello lessons with Lewis were utterly different than they had been with Annette when she started. Beginning cellists should work on their sitting positions, to ensure that good posture is established early, thus preventing future problems. All of the students

I had ever taught ended up having to work on this, either at the beginning or later on. Annette had been normal in this respect, needing many repetitions of sitting with and without the cello until she could do so without twisting. But Lewis sat, I put the cello up to him, and he merged with it. If I was going to use the word "prodigy" to describe a beginner, I would have applied it to Lewis. To me, a major component of musical talent was early mastery of the physical tasks involved. I had watched so many of my students battle, as I myself had done, to transform ourselves from stiff, insecure players into fluid, natural musicians. Lewis appeared to bypass this struggle entirely.

The bow hold is another big challenge for many cellists. I was accustomed to hammering into all my students, especially the young ones, the need for correct, focused repetition. Lewis did have to work on this a bit: I placed his hand on the bow perhaps ten times before he got it. Any teacher of beginners knows this is phenomenal. I was used to Lewis' gift for mastery of all sorts of physical tasks, so I wasn't exactly shocked by the absence of so many struggles that I knew were normal. But part of my brain was always just hopping during his lessons: *He's not going to have to work on that, either? Did he just do what I thought he did? What if I told him to use the bow and left hand together? Already? It's way too soon! He'll get bad habits. But he's not even using a third of his mind; what would happen if I came up with something really hard? Should we start flashcards already? Maybe I should make him sing half and whole steps today. How do I proceed? There's no pedagogy course for this situation!*

So I had to continue to invent my own pedagogy as we went along. I did insist on as much drill and repetition as possible, because I was aware that a young player who moved too fast would probably end up with a shaky technical foundation. But these drills required such a tiny percentage of Lewis' whole mental capacity that I had to become rather crafty, both to get his cooperation for a task so mundane, and to formulate a sufficient challenge for him within the framework of my goal. I was adamant that his bow hold, left hand position, sitting posture, and rudimentary tone production skills all had to reach a certain level before I would allow him to widen his musical horizons. Although he could do these things so easily, he was not consistent. I delayed music reading, but not pre-reading activities that we could do without the cello, such as the blue la flashcards. I knew that if we did this early, he would be in no danger of illiteracy. I tried everything I could think of to get him to slow down so that the onslaught of music reading and more complicated playing tasks would not aggravate the inconsistency in his basic technical skills. But his need for self-determination was overwhelming. Annette's lessons had taught me well, and I was more adaptable this time. When he began asking to read music, an activity I thought too tall for him at this stage, I let him do it.

My attitude was almost slaphappy. After all, I was in the process of tossing out everything I knew about teaching. I thought, *Sure, he's pulled out the most complicated etude book in my stack, why not let him try? There's got to be an open string[1] or two in here.* So we would look through the music, with me calmly explaining all about clefs, sharps and flats, different note values,

---

[1] Open strings are considered easy, and possible for beginners, because while the student is bowing on them, the left hand does not stop the string. For music reading this is also considered suitable for beginners because there are only four possibilities to remember (the cello has four strings).

fingerings, and tempo markings. He drank it all in, and I would show him two notes that he could actually play, then he would play them and be happy. An outside observer, or I at an earlier stage (ten minutes ago) would have fretted, *But this is silly—it's way over his head! He's not getting anything out of this; we need to be clapping simple rhythm patterns or singing nursery songs.* But the point was not that he had to understand every marking on the page, or even every word I said—he just wanted to be immersed in the full complexity of musical study. I found that the more tall activities I let him try, the more he cooperated when we worked on elementary things.

His musical soul was way beyond his technique, and this worked both for and against him. His mind was filled with the music that Annette, all my other students, and I myself worked on. He wanted to play all of it. He sang everything from *Twinkle, Twinkle, Little Star* to snatches of my Bach Unaccompanied Suites. One day he insisted on trying to play *Long, Long Ago,* a piece he had been caroling forth for several days. I knew what was about to happen, but decided not to try to avert it. His ears and his voice knew exactly how *Long, Long Ago* should sound, complete with a clear concept of what sort of tone quality he should produce. When he tried to play it, the first few notes were fine, and then he stalled out because he didn't have the technique to play the piece yet. It was a terrible shock to him. He had been unable to comprehend that a piece that he could hear and sing exactly as it should sound would be so impossible to actually play. He cried and cried, leaving it to me to pick up the emotional pieces. Fortunately, it was familiar terrain: I had lived through many years of this. The disparity between my technique and my musical vision was a horrible frustration, but also a spur toward excellence. One of my primary functions as Lewis' teacher became the providing of empathy, helping him to handle frustration, and pointing the way toward technical mastery.

The other challenge did not abate: that of learning to honor his drives while still retaining enough authority to offer the necessary guidance. Music reading continued far beyond his playing ability, but it was like Annette and the flashcards: it didn't bother him. He'd sit with the cello and bow in his hands, and stare at the page of music, not hearing anything I was saying to him. It didn't concern him in the slightest that he understood only a small fraction of what he was looking at. In fact, that was just what he liked about it. With my capacity for occasionally walking into his brain, I could see what was going on. This was tall, his mental abilities were vast, and that page in front of him beckoned with all sorts of things to learn and puzzles to solve.

But the fact remained that he needed to master beginning music theory and reading, and basic cello technique. At every turn I felt like I was doing battle with his drive to express what he had inside himself that day:

"Lewis, time to work on your left hand position."

"But Mommy, I have a little song that has to come out; may I play it?"

"Yes Lewis, but first you need to work on your left hand a bit. Now put three fingers on the D string."

Sometimes he responded, sometimes not. If not, it was because the "little song that had to come out" had captured his attention completely. I was an impediment, a vague faraway mumbling. This was not something I realized immediately. We had many stormy practice sessions which were not caused by the normal conflicts between mommy and two-year-old. He was brilliant and driven, and sometimes I just had to get out of the way. Before I learned to do this, he and I both suffered in this clash. He was the young genius, I the obtuse instructor.

It was interesting to observe the path that Lewis' cello playing took: so different from Annette's, so driven by his personality. Where Annette had been eager for my guidance, Lewis wanted to brush me aside. Annette was a tractable student, though difficult in her own way, but Lewis knew just what he wanted to do. Both children had a lightning-quick grasp of the abstract concepts involved in music reading, but Annette did not develop the ability to master a physical task after only a few tries until her third year of lessons. We spent those first years in drill and repetition. When Lewis had the music stand in front of him, I worried. Was he really able to keep all of the elements of his playing secure and also occupy his mind with the page of music? He had had so much less time than Annette to lay his technical foundation. He regarded himself as an equal member of the musical community at our house: if we were reading music, he should too. Anything less was "short." To him, the length of time he had been playing before learning to read music was immaterial.

I also had to scramble to keep up with Lewis' emotional needs. This dictated the pace of his learning. I had gained much from working with Annette that I could apply to Lewis, but teaching him held difficulties for which nothing in my previous experience had prepared me. True, I was by then accustomed to improvisation, but I had to step up my pace if I was going to be of any help to him.

Some days I felt like an abject failure, so much so that I wondered if there was any point in continuing. Both children were passionately interested in learning to play, but when we sat down for lessons, I couldn't just flip the switch from "Mommy" to "teacher." Nor did they suddenly become model students because it was time to practice. It was a roller coaster: while Annette was working on her bow hold, she would suddenly begin to act her chronological age. My patience would evaporate, and the lesson was doomed. Lewis' mind could flicker off to something more absorbing and I would fail to realize it for ten or fifteen minutes. Several years passed before I finally understood that these children, with their prodigious minds, were capable of appearing to pay attention, even following directions (albeit badly), while their thoughts were absolutely elsewhere. Much of my ingenuity had to be applied to the continuing problem of preventing boredom in the midst of drills, realizing when I was dealing with my two or four-year-old, not my brilliant student, and adapting to the shifting demands of teaching highly gifted young children—with no prior experience.

On days when toddlerhood predominated over genius, I often felt that I couldn't take it any longer. Tears on both sides were commonplace, especially when I terminated a practice session for lack of cooperation. More than once I threatened both children with getting rid of the cello entirely, and I meant it. At different stages of their cello studies, I actually did halt lessons with both children, each for a period of about a week. This came not from a detached, reasoned decision, but from me being frustrated and fed up. This was not a good way to do things, but I was stuck where I was until I could move on.

These breaks were always productive—the deprived child would begin begging the very next day, I had time to cool off, then we would resume on new terms. After one of these cycles, I could look back and see that it was a requirement for their progress that I insist on change. Over time, I learned to do this in a more preventive mode. However, this didn't alter the fundamental reality: that I was an intense, excitable person dealing with two other creative, brilliant, excitable people who also happened to live in the same house with me all day long. It was a situation charged for explosions. In this context, life couldn't possibly be placid, and I couldn't succeed if success meant smooth forward motion. It was more often a jagged scrawl.

I was glad I had married Ellis Hein, the most soothing person on earth. During our engagement, we spent the 1987 Christmas holidays at my father's house. By the second day my family was driving me wild, and I remember sobbing on Ellis' shoulder. He put his hand on my head, and I felt instantly calm. It was uncanny. I had observed him on his family farm in Oklahoma, and seen that he was skilled, even sensitive, in his handling of the livestock.

Then a few years later I caught him soothing and definitely communicating with wild animals. Sometimes I wondered if I had married "Crocodile" Dundee. But Ellis was not flamboyant. In fact, he was an expert at blending in with the woodwork. I envied him this trait; I found it attractive. My talkativeness had landed me in so many alienating situations that I was ready to learn how to be quiet. But I couldn't; it went against my grain.

However, I have learned other things from being married to Ellis: his convictions are like granite.

He is literally a rock in some important ways. I have watched others make the mistake of thinking that he is a milquetoast because he is quiet. I have watched myself make this mistake. I have learned that when I need sympathy, I get it, but when I need truth, I get that, too. He has one of the most incisive minds I have ever encountered. He is a priceless asset to me in helping sort out all the puzzles of teaching the cello to two brilliant young children.

At the end of the worst practicing days in the early years, I could pour out my woes, and Ellis would begin asking questions. To be with him and to talk to him would clear my mind. Then, together we could craft the solutions our children needed to keep their learning on track. Like Bunter in Dorothy Sayers' Lord Peter Wimsey mysteries, Ellis has "a way with him," and this works in favor of everyone at our house.

5

PREPARATIONS FOR HOME SCHOOLING

We began formal, scheduled home schooling the fall of 1998, when Annette and Lewis were 5½ and 3½. But their academic education had begun a few years before this, because Annette was reading and Lewis was always thinking about numbers.

I'd begun researching home education when Annette was about three years old. I started at the public library again, but this was even more of a disappointment than my search for information about giftedness. I remember finding exactly two books: one was by and for religious fundamentalists, and was primarily an attempt to encourage and reassure the mother that she was capable of the job. The other was *Better Than School,* by Nancy Wallace, and it was fabulous. Its quality helped make up for the scarcity of more books. In her story of home schooling her children she commented that they were not gifted, but I disagreed. Ishmael and Vita Wallace did many amazing things at early ages, and Nancy's description of their household sounded a lot like ours.

However, since I was not yet actively teaching both our children, this book functioned less as an example of how to home school than it did as a source of relief to me that the early home schoolers had paved the way for us to exercise this option free of many legal hassles.

But as for practical advice about how to get started, information about curricula, and how we could find a network of compatible people, I was left hanging. Somehow I got a list of current home schooling periodicals, and sent for sample issues. This was an eye-opener. I had known a few home schooling families who appeared to do nothing; sometimes their children did not learn to read until age eight or older. This horrified me, all the more when I discovered that there were whole periodicals and groups devoted to this approach, called "unschooling." Most of the other magazines were religious in bent, typically featuring on their covers glowing parents with their ten rosy children. I was not very interested in the curricula discussed in these magazines, but read the articles anyway. I found a few other non-fundamentalist periodicals, even one that celebrated "ethnic-racial-religious-philosophical" diversity, but this did not meet our needs. We ended up subscribing to none of them.

I also thought maybe periodicals relating to giftedness would be helpful. Through reference works at the library, I finally found one: it turned out to be by and for public educators, and I could not wade through the jargon. Where was even a scrap of information for parents who were home schooling their gifted children because they did not trust the public schools to do a proper job? Nowhere, apparently.

It did not occur to me to try the Internet. Ellis and I had philosophical objections to it. We owned a computer, but used it for bookkeeping and word processing only. We had read, with disapproval, about people's "virtual" trips to this or that place, and about online discussion groups for every subject under the sun. We did not think that such a huge amount of information was a good thing. We already had too little time together and sensed, correctly, that to join an online discussion group would exacerbate this problem. We also wanted to devote as much time as possible to Annette and Lewis. We saw no good reason to "virtually" invite several dozen or hundred people into our living room when we barely had time to talk to each other.

Besides, I hated computers. I had never really learned to use them, the monitor gave me eyestrain, and if I hadn't been a writer I would never have gone near one. Books attracted me, not technology, so it did not even enter my mind that I could locate the information and support I needed via the Internet.

During those few years before we began formal home schooling, I was haunted by the feeling that we were not doing enough for our children. I had begun to get a faint sense of the huge capacity of both their minds, a capacity demonstrated by their insatiable desire to learn. Often during cello practice, especially near the end, when I was worn out, neither child would want to stop. They acted like they were starving. Even if I had succeeded in challenging them that day, it seemed to stimulate them rather than wear them out. I was the one who was tired. They were two bottomless pits, and I stood on the edge, shoveling at top speed. True, they both had low-energy days, but these were the exception.

Time was also becoming a big problem. I had to confine their practicing to half a day, either morning or afternoon. There was too much to do around the house, and in our work, to allow the cello to invade the whole day. As Lewis' practicing grew beyond the early stages, this created tremendous pressure on me. After breakfast, I would literally rush to clean up the kitchen, accomplish basic grooming chores, agonize about all the other things undone, and begin my daily race to keep up with my children's learning.

We settled into a routine, if you could call it that, where Annette and Lewis took turns getting the first practice session of the day. That time slot was always the longest, and it invariably ran overtime. This left very little for the child who was second in line: that practice session usually ended up being a check-in for the basics at his or her level. For Lewis, it was posture, bow hold and left hand, and for Annette it was review pieces. Then I had to extricate myself, always feeling like I had cheated that child, because he or she was begging to play just one more piece, or to do flashcards, or, in Lewis' case, to disassemble the bow or endpin attachment.

Lunch was often late. Even if we had snacked at the right time, I was hungry again, and therefore unfocused. True, it didn't take a lot of brains to get a meal on the table but it did require some attention, and I was preoccupied. How was I going to get Annette to fix her bow hold? Was Lewis really learning what he needed to by examining my advanced etude and orchestral excerpt books? I would have preferred to spend that time on drill. And what about the house? Dust was the least of the problem. I remembered Audrey Grost, author of *Genius in Residence*. She described the perpetual clutter caused by her son's projects, and commented that few housewives would have tolerated such chaos, but at least it was clean. I couldn't imagine how she had accomplished even that.

I fretted continually about our children's educational needs. Musical study is one of the most demanding activities imaginable for anyone, but especially for a four-year-old and a two-year-old. Their progress had begun to accelerate to the point where I could see the details of their musical development several years into the future, yet realized that these particulars would probably be compressed into a much shorter time span. This made me feel compressed, too. And music was only one of their interests. Every day I thanked God that Annette was reading. Our biggest problem on that front was finding the time to get to the library, and to bring home a big enough stack of books. Her mind was like a vacuum cleaner. I remember one morning when I had arisen early to practice. Annette woke up, brought a new Nancy Drew book to the couch, and speed-read all the way through it in the remaining forty-five minutes of my practice session. Accustomed as I was to her abilities, I still could not believe my eyes. Afterward, I quizzed her on the plot and it became clear that she had read every word.

I worried that she was not well-rounded, and that she needed math and science instruction from us. This was impossible. Our days were packed so full that even we were amazed that we could cope with everything that we had to do.

I was so practiced at making whole grain muffins—and Ellis at baking bread—that we could do these things in our sleep, and just about had to. While chopping interminable piles of vegetables for yet another batch of homemade soup, I longed for my single days when I ate deli meats, canned soups, and even an occasional TV dinner. Back then, of course, I knew better than to eat those things, but was not yet fully alive to the damage that additives, preservatives, and other artificial ingredients inflict on human health.

When we got married, Ellis, who had been raised on a farm, became head cook. He provided such delicacies as fresh tortillas, homemade chicken salad for my lunches at work, and hot, nutritious suppers brought to my office for that rushed half hour on Tuesday evenings between my last student and the weekly Oshkosh Symphony rehearsal. It was a far cry from the days when Tuesday supper had been a single container of Yoplait yogurt.

About six weeks after we were married I found myself at the deli counter in the grocery store asking, "What's the difference between these thin-sliced meats and this large chunk over here?"

The clerk pointed to the haunch of beef and said, "This one doesn't have preservatives."

With a horrible jolt I saw what I had been doing to my body during all those years of eating conveniently sliced—and carcinogenic—deli meat. Although my mother's dietary practices had left their mark on me, I had become so busy with teaching and performing that I had slipped far into convenience food buying.

I went home and gazed at Ellis in delight. Somehow I had found and married a man who was not only a nurturer, but also willing to work long hours just to help us create a superbly healthful diet. Our cooking and eating habits were entrenched by the time the children were born. At that point I had become as committed as Ellis was to maintaining the quality of our diet. Those daydreams about canned soup and deli meat were self-deceptions, and I knew it. If I wanted good health for our whole family, I knew perfectly well that this commitment required that we spend a lot of time in the kitchen.

I had to figure out how to fit in all the chopping, baking, preserving, storing, and other work that our whole-foods, mostly organic diet required. This made the kitchen a tyrant, but it was a conscious choice between the massive time drain of so much cooking and the disastrous effects of saturating our bodies with artificial ingredients.

We also used cloth diapers. I have no recollection of how we survived that one-year period after Lewis was born and before Annette toilet-trained. There must have been a breathing period, of sorts, between the time that Annette was out of diapers and Lewis began the cello.

Of course that stretch of time was devoured by Annette's practicing, which was elastic: as much time as I had, that's how long her attention span was. After Lewis started the cello I had two pieces of elastic to contend with because his curiosity was, if possible, even more voracious than hers. He wanted to know everything all at once, not just about music reading and how to play the cello, but also about musical instrument construction and acoustics. So I spent half-days trying to stretch my efforts thin enough to encompass both children's musical needs—an impossible job. I spent the rest of my time running to keep up with household chores and to stay afloat artistically. I did not have many paying students, and the Wyoming Symphony schedule was minimal by professional standards, but it was all I could handle.

Lewis' needs preoccupied me more than Annette's did at this stage because I had never really adjusted to the idea that he wasn't going to get as much attention from me as Annette had. He would never be an only child. True, he had a big sister who liked to read to him and show him how to write and draw, but I hardly ever read to him, and this distressed me. During the stage at which he could not be torn away from puzzles, I began to relax, both because he was clearly getting what he needed, and because his mind and temperament were so different from Annette's. Nonetheless, I heaved a big sigh of relief when at age three he began reading, because I figured our troubles were largely over.

But it was not to be. Lewis did not take to solitary reading the way Annette did. He loved stories and he loved being read to, but he did not sit and read for hours. In fact, he didn't read much at all. At this point, I started worrying again. He was fascinated with numbers, but if I didn't have time to read to him how was I ever going to be able to sit down with him and do the basic math activities that I was sure he would love?

The occasional counting books I found at the library did not go beyond twenty, and were just not complicated enough to encompass the depth and breadth of Lewis' interest in numbers. I worried about this for months. He was getting tremendous stimulation from cello practice, yet it was not sufficient. I had daily glimpses into the complexity and vast reaches of his mind, and I knew practicing did not fill it. For the educational challenges he needed, the cello was only a beginning.

While Annette's reading habits were a source of reassurance to me, I did have one big worry concerning her. I thought she needed an art tutor. Most of her drawings seemed unremarkable, but she had done a few in her pre-reading years that were outstanding. Some of these I dated and kept, for the same reason people pinch themselves to make sure they are awake. I couldn't believe it at the time, and wanted them for evidence later. One drawing in particular was like the "side" incident—not possible. So I worried and worried about how we were going to find and afford an art tutor.

I did not have much interest in enrolling her in classes because of my own bent toward private teaching. I had seen the counter-productivity inherent in group instruction, and didn't want it for her. I also knew it would be hard to find a superior artist who could also teach, and loved children as well. Such individuals were rare. So I lived in a state of paralysis about this for several years. Being unable to afford a tutor was only part of my dilemma. I held my own teaching to a high standard and expected the same from others, especially anyone who was going to work with my own child. As a young teacher I had gone through that early learning period where I had done many things badly, then looked back and saw how I could have done them better. I knew that becoming a fine teacher was a lifelong process. I wanted to locate someone for Annette who was as advanced along this continuum as possible.

The other issue which troubled me to the point of paralysis was that of basic competence. I knew nothing about visual art, but I knew my philosophy:

that beginners should be taught by the great masters. Who else has the vision and personal experience of the highest levels of creative discovery? Why should the youngest students, just because they are beginners, be denied access to that level of quality? In this respect I was close to one of the basic tenets of the Suzuki approach.

I knew I was up against a concept of education in music, as well as in many other disciplines, that permeates this culture: advanced teachers should be reserved for advanced students. Supposedly, beginners can be taught by almost anyone who has had an introduction to the subject. I saw what this mentality did to beginning string players. Most universities require music education majors to take a one-semester string methods course in which they are introduced to the violin, viola, cello, and bass. Whether or not they are string players, this supposedly qualifies them to teach orchestra, but it does not. Of course I had known many public school string teachers, even wind, brass, and percussion players, who transcended these mediocre requirements; yet the finest string players, if they enjoyed children and liked to teach, could always do a better job.

But how was I to evaluate the skill of a visual artist? I was in the same state of ignorance that I had observed in so many parents of young string players. They selected a teacher on the basis of visibility and/or reputation, but often these factors had almost no connection with that person's competence as a teacher of beginners. I didn't even know how to start my search for that gem of a person who had a passion for excellence combined with the desire to share it with others, even if those others were "just children." I did not know what to do, so I did nothing.

But there was Annette, with all this amazing artistic potential, stagnating for lack of proper attention. She did not act as though she were deprived, but, as with Lewis, I lived with the knowledge that her abilities were so prodigious that it was not humanly possible to tap into all of them.

I knew this, but had not yet succeeded in placing limits on my own expectations. My fretting traveled a cycle of apathy and defeat, climbing up into frenetic, usually unproductive efforts to find ways of providing more for Annette's and Lewis' education. During these outbursts I spent time and money, often unwisely. I would get out a stack of home schooling curriculum catalogs and pore over them, all the while knowing I would not find what I was looking for. Or I would snatch a few minutes during time designated for household errands to visit the local school supply outlet. I was rarely satisfied with what I found, but sometimes made a purchase anyway, only to regret it later. Part of the problem was that many written materials for young learners were so cluttered with cutesy pictures that they practically obscured the core tasks. I also felt that educational materials for Annette and Lewis should be well tailored to their needs, but the search for this was not an easy job.

Two successes stand out from this time: When Annette was 4½ I found a third grade Latin primer and pronunciation tape for her, which she gobbled up. And that same summer, I bought for Lewis, who was 2½, a digital kitchen timer with a clock, a stopwatch, and a second timer. For these four functions, there were two fields of display, and he had to learn to manipulate the buttons to change displays and figure out why some of the numbers counted for-

ward, others backward, and, in the case of the clock,
at different rates. He loved it. It took him about six
weeks to master it. As I watched him pushing the
buttons and working to figure it out, my feelings of
satisfaction were vast.

Our other efforts at serving Lewis' needs were
not as successful. He was so different from Annette
that we felt like novices in most of our dealings with
him. His emotional intensities were always right out
there on the surface. This made it difficult to tell, in
any given incident, whether or not we had crossed
the border between discipline and injustice. He also
did not respond well to interruptions. If it was time
to change his diaper, and he was in the middle of
something else, we had to either bodily haul him off
or engage in a lengthy series of reminders which invariably degenerated into nagging and then punish-
ment.

We expected difficulties during the "terrible
twos," but not to such an extreme. The sheer volume of his protests was the least of it. The reminding, nagging, arguing, disciplining, and self-doubt
were an unremitting energy drain. As he grew older,
toilet-trained, became more able to dress himself and
take on other responsibilities, a new problem arose:
he was often lost in thought. He endured a long,
difficult stretch of time during which we thought he
was an incorrigible dawdler. But this proved to be a
tiny fraction of the truth; and until we realized this,
everybody in the house was unhappy.

Day after day, we reminded Lewis to do this or
that chore; then fifteen minutes later found him
wandering around in another part of the house. We
tried to be patient, but after awhile this was impossible. It became a joke—not a very funny one—about

how many times we had to tell him to do something before he actually got it done. Mornings were the worst, because it took him so long to get dressed and ready for breakfast. I lost my temper often. But yelling and punishing had no more effect than nagging. I felt like the world's worst parent.

Even Ellis, the calm and steady, the quiet and collected, lost patience. It was miserable. I felt worst of all for Lewis, because he obviously needed some sort of help or guidance from us that he was not getting. The household routine began to break down as Ellis and I put an increasing amount of time and energy into this problem, but to no avail. A gimmick that worked one week failed the next. We began to worry that Lewis was incapable of focusing his mind. As time went on, this view seemed to fit his behavior better than the deliberate disobedience we had first suspected.

All children dawdle in resistance to parental authority, and we had seen plenty of this with Annette. But if Lewis was primarily a dawdler, he was in his own league. Our mounting unhappiness, and his, forced us to consider his habits and all we knew of his personality and emotional makeup. By close observation, we finally concluded that he was a daydreamer. We valued daydreaming. We regarded it as essential for creative work, and had discovered that it nourished and cleansed the mind. Our past experience had taught us that thinking, especially solitary thinking, led to ideas, and ideas solved problems. We had plenty of those, and so far our wits had been equal to the task, but wits, like plants, had to be watered and fed. We began to wonder if we were crushing a young and tender sprout. Our approach to discipline was strict; we had a horror of raising ill-

behaved brats. But to know and serve Lewis, we had
to change.

As we proceeded according to our new hypoth-
esis, we made some important discoveries. Upon finding Lewis in the bathroom washing his hands for the
third time when he was supposed to be making his
bed, instead of yelling at him, Ellis or I would ask,
"Lewis, what is going on in your mind that's causing
you to forget about making your bed?"

He'd turn his chubby little 3½-year-old face up
to us and reply, "Did you realize that twenty plus one
is twenty-one, and thirty plus one is thirty-one, forty
plus one is forty-one, and so on?"

"Lewis, what's twenty plus two?"

" . . . twenty-two!"

"Thirty plus two?"

"Thirty-two!"

"Forty—"

"I know, I know, Mommy! Forty-two!"

"Lewis, what's twenty plus eight?"

" . . . twenty-eight!"

"Twenty plus five?"

"Twenty-five!"

"Thirty plus four?"

"Thirty-four!"

"Do you get how this works?"

"Yes, it's so easy. Twenty or thirty or whatever it is
plus all those other numbers is twenty or thirty-what-
ever-it-is . . ."

"Depending on what number you choose to add
to your twenty or thirty."

"Yes, Mommy. That's a very exciting discovery,
isn't it?"

"Yes. Now let's go get your bed made."

Another day, he would be lost in a small snatch

of music that he was singing over and over again. I thought, *He's probably trying to picture the notes on the staff, or maybe figure out the rhythm. But if he doesn't get his pajamas off right now, he'll be late for breakfast and get cranky. Then we'll all be sorry.*

Pulling his attention off of his mental preoccupations was reminiscent of that episode in *Farmer Boy* in which Almanzo's parents were absent from the farm for a week. The Wilder children spent six days making candy, eating watermelon, and neglecting the many summer tasks. Then, while madly rushing about on the last day trying to catch up, they discovered a piece of taffy stuck to the kitchen floor. As with Lewis' attention, no matter how many times they tried to pull it loose or scrape it off, some of it always stuck to the place where it had been.

"Lewis! Stop staring at the Periodic Table of the Elements and eat your lunch!"

I went from thinking *How will he ever learn to focus his mind?* to *Who would want to bother with folding his clothes or eating when his thoughts are so much more interesting?* Of course we knew he'd have to learn to function somehow in the world. It was our job to teach him how, and yet we knew we mustn't discourage the thinking. This was and is a challenge, but one for our wits. Progress in one area dictated sacrifice in another. As Ellis and I took the time to probe Lewis and discuss our findings, that was time subtracted from my practicing, from Ellis' bookwork, or—most often—our sleep. We could ill afford the time, even in the face of restored energy and spirits. And then there was Annette. While she was reading, or rather vacuuming, we were emotionally absent. Would she grow up glued to books and be gone before we realized what had happened? We began to see the necessity for reserving opportunities for each of our children and ourselves, both for times of solitude and for companionship.

But seeing this and accomplishing it were two different things. We had so much more to do than we had time to do it in, that it was another not very funny joke. Ellis and I were on the hundred year plan for renovating our 1917 house. I had beautiful oak cabinets in the kitchen, and designer closets, all without doors. We had two home-based businesses. All sorts of minor and major life tasks routinely went undone, everything from bank statements to birthday cards. We had no time together. But by far the biggest drain on me was the time I spent helping Annette and Lewis with their practicing. I had begun to feel like the cello was a devouring monster, and wondered how much longer I could hold out before I would have to practice with one child in the morning and one in the afternoon.

Ellis frequently suggested that I take a day off from practicing with the children. He was right, but days off happened because of dental appointments, haircuts, and other chores which broke the routine. Also, I had gained much in the past from perceiving music as athletics: it pays to stay in shape, and that requires training. No Sundays off, no holidays, no skips unless you make a conscious decision to take a break. I had made my bed and was thrashing in it. I wasn't exactly burning out; how could I in the face of daily contact with two of the most exciting students I had ever taught? But I was definitely fraying at the edges because of the multiple pressures involved.

During this time I read a bit of sage advice from a home schooling expert: if you don't have time to inform yourself and properly research curricula, you don't have time to home school. My reaction was, "HA!" At times I was sustained only by my conviction that the public schools would do a far worse job than we were doing.

6

MY DENIALS BEGIN TO CRUMBLE

Although I had little interest in the activities of our local school district, I couldn't help noticing that they were discussing the possibility of starting a program for gifted students. I grew curious enough to call the principal that was supporting it, to ask him what they were trying to do. In the course of the conversation he mentioned that at the end of that summer they were holding a two-day conference for teachers and members of the community. The guest speaker was Dr. Linda Silverman, director of a place called the Gifted Development Center, in Denver, Colorado. I had heard of the Gifted Development Center months ago, in a conversation with an acquaintance whose children were also gifted. She had directed me there in response to a question I'd asked her about periodicals. I'd written down the phone number but hadn't found the time to call for information.

When the week of the conference arrived, I had

just returned from a ten-day business trip. In harmony with our unusual approach to food, during the prior year we had discovered the nutritional virtues of blue green algae and had become distributors for a company called Cell Tech. I had driven to Minneapolis, Minnesota, for August Celebration, their annual conference.

It was a worthwhile trip, but it was time during which the children had not practiced. Their vacation had been wonderful but they needed to get back to the cello. If I attended the conference on gifted education, that would be two additional days off for them. Getting back into shape was never fun, so I decided not to attend but to stay home and practice with Annette and Lewis.

As the time drew near, however, I began to have second thoughts. Any decision to leave the house for an additional two days had to include Ellis, and the inevitable financial considerations. We were constantly walking the tightrope between how much money we needed to earn and how much time we could afford to take off from work in order to teach the children and also to serve their educational needs in other ways.

Our financial lives had been both eased and complicated by the onset of the algae business. We could run it from home. I could, and did, stuff envelopes, draft newsletters, and read product information after the children were in bed. In the summer, during their playtime, I could snatch an occasional ten-minute stretch to return a phone call or add to our growing list of ideas for building the business.

If I attended the gifted conference so soon after my return from Minneapolis, we would forfeit much of the freshness and momentum of all that I had gained by attending August Celebration. I would also lose my at-home work time, plus Ellis would get even further behind on his contracting work. Nonetheless, he encouraged me to attend. He was always readier than I to invest; to choose time well spent in favor of money earned.

As I sat on the couch the evening before, trying to decide, I felt both drawn to the conference and apathetic about it. I wanted to go because of the subject, but I was disinterested because the public schools were involved. What could they possibly be doing that would be of any use to me or my family? But my apathy had a deeper source: I was still divided in my view of giftedness. On the one hand, I had a voracious appetite for information about it; on the other, I kept telling myself I didn't need to know anything more. Finally I decided to compromise. I'd attend the morning sessions but stay home in the afternoons to practice with the children.

That first day began a process that was to redirect my entire life. As I listened to Linda Silverman talk about the special problems faced by gifted children, I found myself agreeing with everything she said. The longer she spoke, the more deeply I realized that giftedness is a mixed blessing. This was something I had hardly dared to let myself think. I had pushed it even farther down in my consciousness than those early flickering thoughts about Annette being a genius. The reason was simple: if you're bright, the world is your oyster. You have everything going for you and you will have far fewer problems— especially in school and with later achievements— than most people. Because you have so little difficulty learning things, you will be spared many of the troubles that other people face. You're just plain lucky.

But Linda painted a different picture. As she talked, I realized again why I had stopped telling other people what my children were doing. Instinct had warned me. One of her first points was that the gifted are at best ignored; at worst, attacked. As she observed:

> We have always been a country of rugged individualists, and our differences have been protected by law. We have strong sanctions against persecution and oppression of people of different religions, races, national origins, and those with physical handicaps, but the gifted are still fair game. (Silverman 1998)

> Each time a taunt based on a child's exceptionality (such as "nerd" or "dweeb") is permitted in the classroom or on the playground, each time a highly gifted child is deliberately held back academically, each time a school policy prohibits academic acceleration or continuous progress, we need to ask, "What messages are we giving *all children* about developing talents, about the value of academic achievement, and about intellectual diversity?" The school climate needs to support all students—including the most gifted. We would never allow racial or ethnic slurs to go on unchecked in today's schools, nor would we deliberately thwart the intellectual growth of a child with a disability. Yet, profoundly gifted children

(and their families) routinely must deal with
these issues . . . (Kearney 1993)

This was not a new idea to me, but one I had
been denying ever since those early days. I had been
struggling to convince myself that having gifted children was such a good thing that it shouldn't entail
any problems. And if by chance there were difficulties, I felt I mustn't talk about them because they
weren't really significant. The disabled and the retarded had the real problems. My family and I were
the fortunate ones. But while being thankful and
actually excited about our children's gifts, I had gone
too far and wasted considerable energy trying to pretend that everything was going to be easy. Or even if
it wasn't easy, the problems shouldn't be severe
enough to justify complaints. Of course this attitude
created a conflict within me, between myth and
truth. The truth was that we were isolated and overwhelmed. The myth was that we had brought this on
ourselves by insisting on an impossibly high standard
for educating Annette and Lewis.

This did not break over me in full detail at the
conference. I merely sat there breathing sigh after
sigh of relief. The more Linda talked, the better I
felt. By mid-morning my thoughts had progressed
from *Yes, I agree absolutely,* to *She's just like I am! You
mean there's one other person on this planet who's like me?*

Of course that wasn't strictly true, but there was
Linda, joyously displaying all those personality traits I
had learned to hide. I especially liked the clarity and
directness of her remarks. This trait, blunt speech,
always popped out of me and offended other people,
despite my best efforts to restrain it. But Linda wasn't

offending many people that morning. Or if she was, they weren't arguing with her.

During the discussion period, some interesting points emerged. On the subject of the unpopularity of a special program for the gifted, one person suggested that we call it something else. I'd never had any patience with euphemism, and was just beginning to feel irritated, when Linda smiled and said, "As far as I'm concerned, a rose is a rose is a rose!" I wanted to stand up and cheer. Then another person said, "I don't have any problem with what you are saying about gifted education, but all children should have what you're proposing to offer a few." I agreed. This was the reason that Ellis and I were home schooling. We believed that our children's education should be a good match for their needs.

Linda's reply intrigued me: "But most children can be served in the regular classroom; the gifted cannot." I began thinking about normal children in a normal classroom. Sure enough, most of the activities and material provided the proper stimulus to the majority of the class.

Then I pictured 5½-year-old Annette in a third-grade classroom. If she were there all day, when would she practice the cello? Would the teacher allow her to read high school level books? Who would discuss the questions that resulted from her extensive reading and thinking? Lewis would have little chance in any classroom because he'd probably be thinking about music or numbers—and the teacher's voice would be a vague faraway mumbling. I thought, *Sure enough, the gifted cannot be served in a regular classroom.*

I was impressed by Linda's ability to make a point and stick to it. As the morning progressed, the depth of her commitment to serve the gifted became increasingly evident.

At break time, I thanked her for what she was doing, and mentioned that Ellis and I had two gifted children, and that we had no plans to send them to the public schools. She said, "You really should consider getting them tested." I sensed conviction and a deep level of concern: testing clearly meant something different to her than it did to me. As I drove home for lunch, I had a lot to think about.

I walked into my house overjoyed to see my family and impatient to get started on the practicing. This was a surprise. Since when had I felt like a racehorse at the starting gate? Maybe never. What had become of my frayed edges? My thoughts had suddenly been transformed from *Oh no, how am I going to fit it all in?* to *Yes! This is exactly what Annette and Lewis need, and they're getting it! Thank God they're getting it!* I felt motivated, happy, patient, and understanding. I was filled with empathy, and it was all aimed straight at Ellis and the children.

At lunch I gazed across the table at Ellis and thought about how little time he had for his own woodworking projects. I knew how difficult that was for him because I had no writing time. I began to wonder if I could take on more kitchen jobs so that he could go off to his woodshop and make something beautiful once in a while. For the first time, instead of burdening me these thoughts gave me energy and happiness.

After lunch and nap, while practicing with the children I had a cascade of new teaching ideas. More important, I was filled with gentleness and patience. We had a wonderful afternoon—everybody blossomed.

That evening I tried to tell Ellis what was happening to me; but since I didn't have a full grasp of it myself, I couldn't articulate it. The best I could do was to share with him Linda's written presentation plus some of the literature from the Gifted Development Center which I had picked up that morning. There had not been time to more than glance at this information, but when I did sit down to read it—I was riveted. On one sheet it said, "Is Your Child Gifted?" Below was the usual list of traits,[1] everything from a long attention span to a great sense of humor. But underneath this I read, "Are YOU gifted?"

Me?? I thought. *This is supposed to be about my children.* But I read on: "If many of the above characteristics fit you as a child or if the following characteristics fit you now, you may be an undetected gifted adult who needs more information about issues of giftedness." The list[2] was a revelation:

- a sense of humor and creativity few others understand
- remarkable intuition, insightfulness or perceptiveness
- outrage at moral breaches the rest of the world takes for granted
- greater awareness than others and concern for global issues
- intense empathy and respect for all humanity
- feeling out of step and on a separate path
- ability to juggle many things at once and do them all fairly well

---

[1] See Appendix A
[2] © Linda Silverman 1996. Used by permission.

— a passion for truth and sincerity that may
   lead to loneliness or alienation
— a longing for others who share your
   sensitivity and values

Every item elicited from me a . . . *well* . . . *yes* . . .
or a *Yup!* or a *Dear God, Yes!*

For years I had denied that I had any special abilities. This had been an easy position to support, given the lack of external indications. These included my average cello playing and what I supposed to be my below average writing skills. Certainly my life accomplishments were unimpressive by most people's standards. I was a barely-published writer. My earning power was low. I had not pursued a university career. I was a professional, but my priorities had shifted to include marriage and children. I didn't want to "have it all." Rather, I was determined not to miss the few fleeting years, especially the early ones, during which our children would be at home with us. Plus I was nourished by Ellis' companionship, and so curious about him, even after ten years of marriage, that I wanted to give the maximum time possible to our relationship. These circumstances shaped me into wife and mommy first, musician, teacher, and writer second, and wage earner last.

I never measured my intelligence by the size of my paycheck—in fact, sometimes it seemed to me that there was an inverse relationship. And when I did stumble on evidence of my own brilliance, I ignored it. A few years previously, while practicing I discovered something so astounding that I put my cello down, walked into the kitchen, described my discovery to Ellis, and remarked, "This is brilliant!

I'm brilliant!" Instantly I thought, *No I'm not. What an embarrassing thing to say. How could I be brilliant?*

I was left with the evidence: a new way to manage the bow that produced twice the sound for half the effort. It changed my whole approach to playing and teaching. When I introduced it to one of my students, as she tried it, she actually cried out, "This is so easy! It works so well! It's brilliant!" If my students thought so, why couldn't I accept it?

Even when I had read about underachievement in gifted teens, and in those passages had seen my own high school career, I still managed to keep this whole question at bay. To me, giftedness meant life accomplishments. Yet conspicuously absent from this piece of paper I was staring at were such questions as: Have you been nominated for a Pulitzer Prize? or Are you the president of your own multimillion dollar company?

This list of characteristics and capabilities I was staring at was the first clue I'd picked up on in forty-two years that giftedness and achievement could be two different things.

I read the list to Ellis. We agreed that every item fit us both. There was a more detailed list[3] on another page, accompanied by an advertisement for a journal on adult giftedness called *Advanced Development.* I couldn't tear myself away from this. There was an entire periodical for gifted adults that wasn't aimed at Fulbright Scholars? I read and read that longer list. I must have gone over it a dozen times. It was, unmistakably, a list of personality traits, not achievements. For once in my life, I did not think, *There must be some mistake. They can't be talking about me.*

---

[3] See Appendix B

Certain items hit so hard that I felt as if I was meeting myself for the first time: "Do you feel driven by your creativity? Do you thrive on challenge? Do you feel overwhelmed by many interests/abilities?" Two summers ago, when Annette was 3½ and Lewis 1½, I had written the first draft of a book on cello practicing. I couldn't help it. Where had the energy and drive come from for that project when I was so busy and worn out, with one child already playing the cello and the other still in diapers? Did I thrive on challenge? Less than a month after Lewis' birth, I rehearsed the Elgar Cello Concerto with the symphony, to help them prepare for their guest artist. Somehow I had played well enough not to disgrace myself. As the questions on that sheet of paper inquired, did I feel overwhelmed by many interests/ abilities? Well, I had been juggling music and writing since early adulthood. I had a list of about ten years' worth of books I wanted to read. I was curious about math: why I was so bad at it, and whether or not I could ever untangle the confusion which dated from my grade school years. And now the challenge of teaching my own musically gifted children had grabbed me. Yes, the list fit.

Ellis had no trouble believing this. He had never doubted his own abilities or mine, but I had always thought of him as brilliant and me as average. So while I was struggling to accept this new idea, he was, as always, waiting for me to catch up. That night, he wanted to sleep and I wanted to talk. Finally I settled down, but with so much to think about that rest seemed a waste of time.

7

WE DECIDE TO HAVE
THE CHILDREN TESTED

The second day of the conference was even more interesting than the first. I arrived in a state of high anticipation, and soon was happier and more excited than I had ever been.

I listened to Linda speak about the distinction between "gifted" and "academically talented." By definition the academically talented do well in school. The gifted may or may not. Because of their unique educational needs coupled with multiple sensitivities, the gifted often face struggles that others know nothing about. As Linda talked on, I began to feel her deep compassion for the gifted. I was still grappling with the concept that giftedness and achievement were not identical. I knew many people who had great regard for those who had distinguished themselves in some way, but little or no use at all for those who had not. I'd been on the receiving end of this attitude many times: I was insignificant because my achievements were, in the context of the "greats," of comparatively small significance. But to Linda, every gifted person was significant.

She pointed out to us that the gifted comprise two percent of the general population, then presented many statistics establishing that they are a group at risk. It added up to a chilling picture: "A study of the juvenile courts in Colorado revealed that over one-fourth of the delinquent population was composed of students in the top 15th percentile in intelligence and *15 percent of these delinquents were in the top 3 percent of the nation intellectually.*" (Harvey and Seeley 1984) "A government report indicated that a large portion of our drop-outs are gifted." (Marland 1972) "One study conducted at 129 high schools revealed 42 cases of suicide attempts, 8 of whom (19 percent) were identified as gifted students . . . (Hayes and Sloat 1990). Harkavy and Asnis (1985) found that almost 9 percent of the students at a high school for the gifted reported at least one suicide attempt . . . It is speculated that gifted youth are high risks for suicide because of their unusual sensitivity and perfectionism." (Delisle 1986), (Silverman 1989, Silverman 1993, 82). Linda was discussing people who had messed up their lives, or who had come to despair for whatever reason. She was talking about society's losers with understanding and compassion.

I had committed no crime except professional and financial underachievement, but I felt this same understanding flowing from her out to me and to everyone else in that room. This fit with the information I had read the evening before: Linda and her staff at the Gifted Development Center were interested in serving the gifted. Whether their clients were winners or losers was immaterial. This idea was so huge and so new that I had only begun to assimilate it.

I had no such problem with the other concept under discussion that morning: perfectionism. For years I had known that I was a perfectionist. I practiced my scales, etudes, and pieces endlessly, yet they were never good enough to satisfy me. While writing I continually asked myself, Is this exactly what you want to say? Have you said it clearly enough? If the answer was no, I always worked until satisfied, or until I couldn't see how to improve it further. These efforts were alternately fun and frustrating. Either way, I persevered because I was driven to excel, to transcend my own limitations.

Nobody could dispute the value of these efforts. And where my perfectionism did seem arbitrary or pointless, I might have wondered about it occasionally, but it never troubled me.

In pre-computer days, if I left a period or comma out of a business letter, I always typed the whole letter again. Even when a little voice inside of me said, *Oh, come on! The outcome of this letter will not change one iota if you just correct it by hand,* I replied to myself, *Yes, but . . . well . . . I just have to do it over.* I didn't really know why.

Years later I wrote to the editor of a periodical for permission to quote at length from a back issue. Her response included questions about who I was and what I wrote, because "We're always looking for material from a variety of perspectives." I was glad that the habit of writing perfect letters was so ingrained. From that point forward I had a reply for people who said, as they had many times, "Oh Becky, you're such a perfectionist. Can't you lighten up a little?"

Sometimes they said it in genuine concern, more often with disapproval. I had developed calluses, as it were, against these inevitable remarks. Besides, I'd noticed a small group of individuals in my life who were also perfectionists and who valued this trait in me and in themselves. Many were cello students; a few were colleagues or friends. These were people with whom I had really clicked, especially the students. I had always thought it was a coincidence that they were exceptionally bright. But if I was on my way to accepting the truth about myself, I would have to concede that it was no coincidence at all, but pure logic that one bright person would attract others.

Perfectionism is part of the whole kaleidoscope of personality traits which characterize giftedness. I had never denied this part of myself, but it was a new experience to be told directly, This is you, and it is good! Apparently many of those attending the conference shared my feelings, because there was a long discussion about it. This was my first experience with a group of people among whom it was okay to speak freely about issues relating to giftedness. Even so, when Linda asked for a show of hands from those of us who believed that our children were gifted, only a few of us raised our hands. Then she said, "and which of *you* in this room is gifted?" I sneaked my hand halfway up, then quickly put it down. One other person did the same. Linda had been talking about societal repression of the gifted, and she had made her point. If we felt barely able to acknowledge our children's special abilities in that safe environment, and almost entirely unable to admit our own, where did that leave us with society at large?

That day, I returned for the afternoon session. I had to. After a lifetime of starvation, I'd found a person I had never met before who knew me better than I knew myself. And I had an accepting environment, however temporary, in which to experience that novelty. As that second day came to a close, I realized that many of my views had changed. More than that, I had changed. The whole thrust of Linda's message had been that the gifted are different, and it damages them to be made to fit in. They have emotional, physical, moral, and spiritual sensitivities which increase the potential for serious harm, and they are a special needs population on an equal par with the other end of the intelligence spectrum in their requirements for early assessment and intervention. I knew it now, and went home thinking: *We've got to get these children tested.*

There followed a period of deep introspection, during which I looked back and saw how well we had been serving our children. It had been so easy to focus on what we weren't able to do, because no matter how much we taught them they always wanted more. But after all the discussion about the special learning needs of gifted children, I could see that musical study was perfect for them because it challenged them on many levels simultaneously.

A good musician must learn to play the instrument—a physical task. Deciphering the printed page is a rigorous mental activity. The best music awakens deep emotion in both player and listener; how does the performer learn to pull cold chills out of an audience? Masterworks of music inspire others, filling them with a sense of awe and humility. How can the musicians, who are the interpreters, chart their artistic lives so that they can participate in this process of re-creating a work of genius in sound? Technique, intellectual mastery, musical insight, and the ability to communicate through the cello—this was the project of a lifetime which I was passing on to my children. The potential for growth was infinite in each of these areas: physical, mental, emotional, and spiritual. In my newborn self-awareness, I realized why, despite several attempts to quit, I had stayed with the cello all of my life: I craved challenge, and musical study created it in abundance.

The deep satisfaction I experienced that fall when practicing with the children helped to mitigate my increasing sense that I was trying to do the impossible. I thought, *I can't keep doing this! There isn't enough time! How can I squeeze it all into half the day? What will we do if I have to start teaching one in the morning and the other in the afternoon?* I felt squeezed not just for time but also for depth within those practice hours. I knew that Annette and Lewis would blossom under yet more detail about music theory and cello technique. I had to live with a constant picture of how little we were doing compared with how much more they could absorb. So, on the one hand I felt the best I ever had about their practicing; on the other, I was battling frustration all the while.

During this period, Annette's practicing began to slip in some indefinable ways. I wondered what was wrong, but couldn't figure it out. I was nagging her all the time, usually about her bow hold. I'd grown more adept at perceiving when her mind had begun to wander, and was learning to change tactics more quickly at these junctures, but even this had ceased to work. I began to wonder if she needed more independence in her daily practicing. Such an idea would not have occurred to me before the conference—she was only 5½, and never in my Suzuki teaching days had a child that young been ready to practice by herself. But I had learned much from Linda about the importance of honoring each child's individual needs, and not being misled by assumptions based on chronological age. So, one day I suggested to Annette that she practice by herself. She jumped at the chance. We agreed that for the coming week she would practice alone, and have one lesson with me, just like my paying students did.

Our experiment worked beautifully. She was so excited to be independent and responsible for her own musical growth that I kicked myself for not doing it sooner. But I was a mommy. Sending her off with the cello, unsupervised, was as traumatic as the first time we had let her ride her bike around the block by herself: there went our baby!

Years of teaching had given me deep respect for the incorrigibility of bad playing habits, and I didn't want to undo a bunch of mistakes Annette might teach herself over the course of a few days. But I had to let her go. It was past time to move on, and my unconscious efforts to hold her back and somehow keep her safe were damaging her.

That first morning Annette practiced by herself, I felt a delicious sense of leisure and space. I would practice with Lewis for an hour, or even a bit longer, then the remaining time before lunch would be at my disposal. I had visions of making long overdue phone calls, of writing a letter or two, and maybe even tackling the bank statements. I actually did have about an hour that morning after Lewis and I glutted ourselves on music reading, flashcards, singing, and everything else we could think of. We weren't used to having the whole morning.

My fantasies continued throughout the day. Was I really going to have more time in which to accomplish basic household tasks? *Yes!* I thought, *This will be great! Maybe I'll even get to read a book!* But underneath all my pictures of a clean, organized house and time to myself, reality prodded at me. I knew Lewis. I knew that his practicing would soon vacuum up my imagined extra hour. Sure enough, it took about three days, then we had both adjusted to longer practice sessions and had no trouble filling them. The old tension was back, that impossible ratio between how much he could learn and how little time I had in which to deliver it. This, I began to understand, was life with gifted children.

I stole time in the evenings to read and re-read the material from the conference. It was my sustenance. I had found no better source of information about my children and myself, and could not get enough of it. The Gifted Development Center carried a large selection of articles, books and tapes. I desperately wanted these, especially the books. Most of all I wanted *Advanced Development,* the journal on adult giftedness. However, we were giving serious consideration to having both children tested, and that was going to cost more than a thousand dollars. We were also facing home school related expenses and the purchase of a bigger cello for Annette. Any sort of luxury spending was out of the question. But I felt like I might suffocate without access to more reading material, so one evening, in pure desperation, I ventured onto the Internet.

About six months prior to this, when we had become Cell Tech distributors, we had renounced our principles and added e-mail service to our computer activities. Years before, we had gone through a similar radical shift when we purchased an answering machine. Both of these events had left our friends giggling at us, since they knew all about our opinions. These forced turnabouts had not reduced our dislike of technology, but we had established a love-hate relationship with it.

For me and the computer, it was mostly hate. I knew so little about the Internet that Ellis had to show me every step. Once we had found the Gifted Development Center website, there was a small amount of new material, which I printed out. I also explored a few links to other websites, but this was cumbersome and unproductive, so I emerged from the experience with most of my opinions reinforced. I loved books. I could just pick one up and read it without any stupid pushing of buttons, illogical instructions, flickering screen, or multiple things to malfunction. Most of all I never needed to yell to my long-suffering husband for help. I was not going to take a computer class, and refused to waste my time reading the manual. Ellis put up with a lot from me this way.

Among the many services offered by the Gifted Development Center was telephone consultation. We decided that this might be a good place to start before having the children tested. It was relatively inexpensive, could provide more information about the children and possibly quiet this raging need I had for more contact with these people.

Before the "dialog," as they called it, we completed a seven page developmental questionnaire for each child. This was fun, entertaining, and time-consuming. I was the driving force behind this project and did much of it myself, but with Ellis' full support. He also wanted to take part in the dialog, and so we scheduled it and the day arrived.

We spoke with Betty Maxwell, Associate Director of the Gifted Development Center. The discussion centered on our efforts at serving the children's educational needs. One of my biggest concerns was how we fit, or rather how we did not fit, into the local home schooling support group. Many of their activities were restricted to specified grade levels. At age 5¾, Annette was more than ready to participate in a third through fifth grade spelling bee. I had not the faintest idea how to approach the home schooling group, or even whom to approach, with the request that Annette be allowed to participate. I asked Betty about this, and she replied, "Well, that is an achievement-oriented activity. She shouldn't do it unless she really wants to. What she should be doing is pursuing her areas of interest."

When I heard this, a light went on. I had begun to adjust to the idea that I could be gifted and not eminent. But for the children's academic pursuits, I had not yet separated the concept of learning from testing and competing. I had a sudden vision of their school years being the leisurely exploration of any and all subjects they wished, in privacy and at their own pace. This idyllic picture included the time to really dig in and master a subject. Learning the facts would be just the beginning. Thinking and reflection would follow until they reached the zenith of intellectual challenge: original ideas. This being so valuable, why would we want to clutter up their time with academic competitions? We would pursue this only if they decided to. All of this flashed through me in a big AHA!! and I missed barely a word of the next part of the conversation.

Ellis was talking about Lewis' need to be tall and the frustration it caused him. Betty suggested we include him in whatever household jobs he could learn—anything and everything. Safety, not his chronological age, should be our primary criterion. This fit with all I had learned about the way in which gifted children should be treated. Too often we had tried to limit Lewis' activities around the house because he was so young, but in fact there was no reason why he should not be more fully involved.

This idea of including the children in more of our own activities was not limited to our day-to-day work. When I told Betty how frustrated I was over having no time in which to do fun things like finger painting and puppet shows, she said, "Present them with your dilemmas and ask for their ideas." In other words, we should involve them in our problem solving and thinking, as well as with our physical activities. This was a new and rather shocking idea. They were preschoolers. Should we really be treating them like they were years older? But of course their mental capacities were far ahead of their chronological ages and that was the reason we were seeking expert advice. We had come to understand that our circumstances were not normal. I knew that Betty was not telling us to treat them like miniature adults. Her suggestions were geared toward Ellis and me becoming more flexible and alert to daily opportunities for including Annette and Lewis at a level appropriate to their cognitive processes. This made sense, although it required again that Ellis and I change our approach to child-rearing.

Another concern I shared with Betty was that we never seemed to have enough time, materials, or resources to serve the children's educational needs. I still had the recurring feeling that we weren't doing well enough. But she replied, "On the contrary, I think you're doing an excellent job." This surprised me until she began reading some of the items to us from the developmental questionnaires which we had sent. I had to concede that the children's progress was impressive. This led to my next question, "How gifted do you think they are?" Betty replied, "They appear to be in the profoundly gifted range." We were running out of time, and I didn't have a chance to find out what "profoundly gifted" meant. But I did ask, "From everything I've read, this therefore means that Ellis and I are in the same category?" Her response was, "Almost certainly. These things don't come from nowhere." And with this information I had to be content.

8

WE VISIT THE GIFTED DEVELOPMENT CENTER

After the dialog, I was more certain than ever that we needed to get the children tested. I had no trouble convincing Ellis of this:

"We need to go to Denver to have the children tested."

"At the Gifted Development Center?"

"Yes."

"Okay."

"It's going to cost a lot, at least six hundred dollars per child."

"Okay."

"It'll mean raiding the savings account."

"That's all right."

"We're both going to lose work time."

"I know."

"What if you're in the middle of a job?"

"I'll manage."

"Why are you so willing to do this? I thought perhaps you'd argue. It's going to be expensive, plus you didn't meet Linda or hear her speak."

"Do Annette and Lewis need to be tested?"

"Absolutely!"

"Then we do it."

So I called the Gifted Development Center to set up an appointment. This involved discussion with the staff about which tests were appropriate, and whether or not we should have both children evaluated. We finally decided to have Annette tested, but not Lewis, since he was then only three years, eight months old.

We knew nothing about the recommended tests, and had to rely on the expertise and judgment of the Gifted Development Center staff. I knew only that the assessment included a post-test conference with Linda Silverman. After having met and spoken with her, I knew that her personal advice would be well worth the extra money it would cost. I was also undaunted by the 500 mile round trip from Casper to Denver, the missed days of practicing, school, and work, plus all the other sacrifices involved.

As the time drew near, I became more and more excited. What were we going to learn from this? What sort of place was the Gifted Development Center? What was the rest of the staff like? Most of all, were they really competent? Would we get an accurate picture of Annette's abilities?

The appointed day arrived and we found our way to the Center. After turning Annette loose with her tester, Gretchen Lucas, we gave the morning over to the care of Lewis and the exploration of this facility which was devoted to the service and study of gifted children and adults. It was a small building, but crammed with information and activity. The children's play area contained many toys appropriate for advanced young learners. I was impressed. It was so unlike the usual junk I'd seen in toy stores. The waiting room held the Center's lending library, informational flyers about everything from distance learning to competitions, and, best of all, office copies of *Advanced Development.* We also had a chance to look at some of the books and articles advertised in the promotional literature I had drooled over for so long.

I was so excited I had trouble focusing. What was most important—to gather and absorb as much information as possible about resources for the children, or to glut myself on *Advanced Development* and other reading material? All my life I had been lost in the desert without even knowing it, and here was my oasis.

The morning passed quickly. We saw Annette during her snack break, and she appeared to be enjoying herself. At lunchtime, with all the tests completed, I asked Gretchen if she had gained enough information to tell Ellis and me what we needed to know. She smiled and said, "Oh yes. You'll hear all about it tomorrow."

I had no idea what to expect at the post-test conference, which was scheduled for the following afternoon. That day, having left the children with my aunt and uncle, we decided to arrive at the Center early, in order to get in as much reading as possible. When it was time for the conference, Linda came to the waiting room to get us. She asked, "Did Gretchen say anything to you yet about the test results?" I replied, "No, only that we would get them at this conference." Linda smiled and said, "Well, hang on to your hats!"

I was about to cross the threshold into another dimension of my life, one that I could never have imagined or believed. But I had no clue that this was about to come upon me. I only remember thinking, *Do they really know what they're doing? I suppose Annette is about 130 IQ or something like that. But will the tests show it?*

The news which we received at this conference was so shocking, so stunning, that I do not remember the sequence of events. I know that Gretchen had administered two IQ tests, one called the Wechsler Preschool and Primary Scale of Intelligence (WPPSI-R), the other called the Stanford-Binet L-M. She went over every detail of both tests, including each question with Annette's response. Linda called our attention to a sixty-point disparity between the two test scores, explaining that the Stanford-Binet had a higher ceiling and that this score should therefore be considered the more accurate one.

As I tried to follow Linda's explanation about the way in which Annette's IQ was derived from her test score, I found myself wishing that I had paid more attention to IQ derivation when I'd read those few unsatisfactory library books. However, I had somehow ignored most of what I'd read on this subject in all the years previous to this moment. Denial had competed with curiosity all that time, stomping out my memory for and interest in the most important details to which I had exposed myself. Those details, combined with my daily observations of Annette's abilities, might have at least partially prepared me for the bombshell that was about to drop. Annette's IQ, Linda said, was " . . . , or higher," naming a number that was so staggering that I wasn't sure I had heard right.

Did Ellis and I sit there in total stupefaction? Did we begin asking questions immediately? Did Linda talk? I cannot sort out the sequence of events. But I do remember asking, "What do you mean, 'or higher?' How could it be 'higher'?" Linda replied that IQ tests have a ceiling effect wherein the test is not designed to measure abilities above a certain level. Apparently, it was the equivalent of trying to gauge the height of a person six feet tall, using a five-foot measuring tape. You know that person is taller than your measuring device, but you don't know how much taller—nor do you have a way to determine this.

But this was not the center of the discussion. We talked mostly about Annette's educational needs and how to serve them. Linda encouraged us in our home schooling efforts. She said, "She's so bright that no school could serve her, not even if they have a program for the gifted. She needs one-on-one instruction—tutors and mentors." Linda also said that we should not hesitate to provide her with college level reading material, and "just be sure to explain the words she doesn't understand."

I took in all this advice, but it came as points of light stabbing into a fog. I was in shock. There were so many things to grapple with all at once. I hadn't even known that an IQ of this level was humanly possible. I had observed that Annette was bright, even phenomenal, but the actual measurement of it (however faulty), was just too much to grasp. Because I came from a family of early, avid readers, because Ellis was so bright, because Annette's accelerated development had seemed so natural, it had never occurred to me that she could be this far away from the norm.

Throughout the conference, I struggled to absorb all the information and advice. We needed it. To serve Annette, we were going to have to tap into every available resource. I kept thinking, *Is there anybody out there who even knows how to begin on a task like this—educating someone with a mind of this magnitude?* Sure, we could throw her to the wolves—just send her off to public school, but we were interested in really providing her with an education. These and other thoughts blew across my mind like clouds driven before a strong wind. I tried to keep the thread of the conversation, but time and time again I lost it. I was reeling from the impact of two bombshells: the news about Annette and the news about me. I had read enough to know that the experts regarded giftedness as hereditary. Annette's having been identified as profoundly gifted probably meant that Ellis, Lewis, and I were all in that same range of intelligence. I asked Linda about this, and her answer left no room for doubt. Although I had resisted expert advice all my life, in this instance I could summon up no argument.

At the end of the conference, Linda said, "You have received a stunning piece of news. Had you just been told that your child was profoundly retarded, you would be going through the same process of shock, assimilation, and acceptance. This is going to take some time." She was right. I remember the drive back to my aunt and uncle's house, the evening spent with them, and the trip home the next day, as one in a stupor. I couldn't get my mind around it. That is, I could, with relative ease, accept the news about Annette (and Lewis and Ellis), because I saw the evidence every day. But I had spent forty-two years thinking that I was ordinary, or perhaps slightly above average. There was no room in my self-concept for "genius." It wouldn't fit. But as the days went by, and as I read the stacks of literature we'd been given at the post-test conference, I began to see the truth and yield to it.

9

BARRIERS . . . AND FREEDOM

That journey to the Gifted Development Center was the most isolating event of my life. We told no one of Annette's test scores, not even our closest relatives. All I could think was, *This is news and we don't want to be in the papers.* Some members of my family could not keep a secret, and others would be scornful, I knew. Ellis had many nieces and nephews, and there was no point in announcing to anyone that we had a bona fide genius in the family. When my father asked me what we had learned from Annette's tests, I replied, "We found out that she is gifted." A disingenuous answer, but I had nothing else to offer.

I had even less to say to the other people in my life: friends, acquaintances, and colleagues. Those who knew of our recent trip asked how it had been. Usually I said, "Oh, fine," and left it at that. We had told a handful of people our reason for going, and these few were naturally curious about what we had learned. I couldn't tell them. If we weren't even going to share information with the children's grandparents, how could we divulge it to anyone else? Few people pressed for details, but when they did I developed a stock answer: "If I told you her IQ, your jaw would drop to the floor, your eyes would bug out of your head, and you would accuse me of lying." People had to accept this, but of course it only piqued their curiosity.

At the same time I was having these conversations, my inner life was exploding. It was a happy event, yet one I could only discuss with Ellis and one other close friend. I couldn't imagine saying to anyone else, "Yes, we've recently discovered that Annette is even brighter than we thought she was. In fact, she's a genius." By itself this remark would have brought guffaws from certain quarters. We were used to the necessity of being tight-lipped about our children's abilities. As parents of gifted children, we knew that merely by stating the facts, we would be perceived as bragging. This difficulty had not changed, but it had intensified.

About my own awakening, those who would sneer at my use of the term "genius" when applied to my children would laugh me out of the room if I dared to label myself as one. I didn't dare, and didn't even want to, but there was no penalty for thinking. I had so much to ponder all at once that I became quite absent-minded in daily life. I began to realize where Lewis got his tendency to drift away from routine activities.

At the post-test conference we had touched on the subject of Ellis' and my inability to fit in with society, and the reason for it: no doubt we had high IQs and therefore were far removed from the norm. Over the years I'd found myself wondering, Why can other people do that, and I can't? What's their secret? How do they do it? Two of the most painful mysteries were about friendship and employment. Less agonizing but as significant were my refusal to pay attention to the news, and my inability to weather a trip to the local pizza parlor. Ordinary things that everyone else could do with apparent ease, I could not or would not do.

I had turned my back on the media when Annette was born. Parents of babies don't have time to open a newspaper, and when I was up and around the house I had no desire to turn on the radio. I sensed that I should not expose Annette to the daily out-pouring of carnage and human folly which goes un-der the name of "news." As she grew older and ac-quired her language skills, I felt this even more strongly. After two or three years of ignoring almost all forms of popular media, I began to wake up to some important facts about myself.

I had known for a long time that when I did lis-ten to the news, I paid a price. Any report of vio-lence stayed with me for days. The more graphic it was, the deeper it went. I reacted the same way to scenes of violence in movies and books. I couldn't stand it. My mind was capable of picturing in far too much detail just what emotional and physical sensa-tions the victims must have suffered. I couldn't keep it off. I learned to choose my books and movies care-fully, but I was much slower to understand that I must do the same with the news. I had internalized the myth that to be a good citizen I had a responsibility to inform myself about the global and national events which the popular media deemed significant. That most of it was bloodshed and injustice was something

I simply had to accept. I could not. During the years prior to my break with the media, I noticed how much shock and emotional damage I sustained on a daily basis, just from having turned on the radio that morning. I had to fight it off all day; and if it was really bad, it stuck for weeks, months, or, in some cases, years. I had begun to understand that this was no way to prepare myself to serve the world, but the pressure to be well-informed was fierce.

After Annette was born and I quit paying attention to the news, I noticed how peaceful my inner life had become. Spared from that daily barrage, my mind was free to reach out, stretch, and relax. Despite the physical and emotional stresses of caring for a newborn, I felt an inner sense of freedom. I came to enjoy the landscape of my thoughts and feelings as never before. This unsullied adventure into my own interior was a source of nourishment and rest I never would have experienced had I continued to punish myself with the news. It felt as though I had been released from prison. I was quick to realize that from a place of inner abundance and peace, I might actually be in a position to give something to somebody else. In the shell-shocked condition I had been in before, that was impossible.

The clearing of my mind had important consequences for my creative work as well. Without the carnage and pain of the world upon me, I could think. I could have ideas. I could explore them. I could discover things, and I did. My cello practicing and teaching, which in tandem had consumed my life from age sixteen to thirty-six, finally began to take off. One day I was helping yet another student through the same difficult passage in a piece that I'd been teaching for years. I thought, *Why is this section so hard? Why does everyone have the same problem with it?* Actually I knew the answers to both of these questions.

That section of the piece was difficult because it lay in the cello's middle range. Everyone had the same trouble with it because the middle range of the cello is a neglected area. Beginners start in the lower registers of the fingerboard (low in pitch; back by the head and shoulder), and get a lot of practice with it before moving on. Cellists have long thought the upper pitch registers (high in pitch, down towards the floor) to be difficult, hence the pedagogy for this part of the fingerboard is prolific.

As soon as I realized that this chronic problem shared by all my students was a basic lack of familiarity with the cello's middle range, the solution popped into my head complete and ready to teach. My students simply needed to practice a three-note exercise in three different combinations throughout the lower and middle range of the fingerboard. I nicknamed this exercise "finger patterns," and began teaching it immediately.

It worked. My most diligent student improved her command of the fingerboard in a few months. She then auditioned successfully for All-Northwest Orchestra, a select regional group for high school students. This was just the beginning. Within a few years, almost all of my students were commenting that they could read fast, complicated passages easily because they saw those three basic patterns which had become second nature to them, and which comprised about ninety-eight percent of all that their left hands would ever have to do on the fingerboard.

Finger patterns, per se, were not a brilliant discovery, much less my personal invention. Finger patterns in various forms are as old as the art of stringed instrument pedagogy. My better teachers had assigned them to me. They appeared in numerous method books, old and new. There was nothing unique about them. However, the effectiveness of my approach to finger patterns lay in my application of them. My students did them by ear, daily. I insisted that they practice them slowly—and for a period of years—far beyond the point where they could do them easily and in tune. This process taught their left hands to function as a portable keyboard all over the cello. In one to three years, they learned a skill that it had taken me twenty years or more to master.

This discovery was one of many yet to come. All followed the same process. First I pondered a problem, then I tinkered. These efforts always culminated in a whole, new, teachable solution which came to me in a single flash. For twenty-eight years my musical life had been on the runway, and suddenly I was flying. I was undisturbed by my lack of eminence—nobody was going to pay attention to my discoveries except my students. They did, and they benefited. I was so excited by the practical applications of my creative musical endeavors, that it was easy to forget that I had little or no credibility in the profession. That didn't matter. The discovery of better ways to play the cello mattered.

As Annette and Lewis grew, I had more time during the brief period before Lewis began his cello lessons, and I started writing again. The same thing happened. I had space in my mind which the news had vacated, and this soon began to overflow with ideas. It was a wonderful awakening, and having reached it I was not willing to drug myself with the fear and pain of the world ever again.

When my education about my own giftedness began, this was one of my earliest insights. I had read, and observed in my own children, that the gifted are physically, emotionally, and morally sensitive. What bothers them, other people are able to tolerate, or may not even notice. The greater the gift, the greater the sensitivity. This solved the mystery about me and the news. How could so many other people live with detailed daily knowledge of the sad state of the world without it destroying them? Well, if I was as far removed from the norm as my children were, the answer was simple: I couldn't stand it, and others could. I was cursed (or blessed) with such a level of receptivity that everything got in, and once it was in, I couldn't get it out. I had no defenses. I still don't have any, nor do I expect to develop them. I was born without this important equipment, and cannot acquire it.

When this piece of the puzzle clicked in, I felt an enormous sense of relief. I was different, and it was okay. It was me. I was not like other people, and there was a good explanation for it. With this realization came an outpouring of energy such as I had never known. In awe I watched as my whole life began to turn around.

This amazing discovery was dwarfed by another even more significant: the reasons behind Ellis' and my commitment to be self-employed for life. My history as an employee appeared excellent, but under this veneer it was fraught with pain. I had left three jobs and one branch of my career for the same reason: there was injustice in the workplace and I couldn't stand it.

As a college undergraduate, I had struggled to repress this trait. While playing in student orchestras under conductors who were abusive, patronizing, or simply boorish, I fought my urge to take my cello and walk out of rehearsal. I needed that conductor's good will for a grade or a letter of recommendation or both. In this way, school was a good preparation for the tyrannies of employment. I passed this test in college, but failed it in adult life. I found that I could tolerate injustice for a while, but then something inside of me would stand up and flatly state, *This is wrong. I'm not going to do it anymore.* And so I would leave that job. During my brief university teaching career, I observed the abuses of the tenure system firsthand. I was never on a tenure track, but had colleagues who were, and I saw what they faced. On the surface, the tenure-granting process appeared to be a fair, merit-based opportunity to earn job security through proving one's competence. But in reality, getting your colleagues to vote for you required a long, delicate dance across a carpet of eggshells.

I only lasted four years in my one-year renewable contract position. Near the end of that time, I unwittingly incurred the wrath of a few key colleagues. Had I been on a tenure track, I knew how it would have gone from there. At that point in my life, a doctorate was the next logical step, but I couldn't do it. To me, the tenure process amounted to hazing: first you go through it, later you do it to other people. When I saw this, that same old part of me stood up and said, *I can't do this, and I won't.* I couldn't and wouldn't grovel. I couldn't and wouldn't risk becoming first a victim and then a perpetrator of those very crimes I would have suffered. Here was another case

of wondering, How do they do it? Some of my ten-
ured colleagues were fine people—they had kept
their passion for their work and were fair-minded.
But many more were petty and lazy. Which would I
become? I didn't want to find out.

After leaving two jobs under horrible circumstances, and watching Ellis go through it once, I knew
that we were both jinxed. I didn't understand it; I
only saw that it kept happening. We had to be self-
employed. This suited us perfectly, except that
money was always a problem. Our skills all lay in highly
competitive, low-paying endeavors. Early on, I worried and tore at this wound of our inability to work
for other people. Why did it always go so wrong? How
could other people stand the workplace, when it had
almost destroyed us? How did they do it? Were we
actually jinxed, or should one of us try it again? The
money would have helped. But I knew It would happen: The Disaster of pouring ourselves into a job only
to emerge sooner or later, halfway toward a nervous
breakdown. But why? Why did we lack this important life skill? There was no answer. I finally concluded that employment was a grinding, crunching
maw for nearly everyone—it was just that they could
stand it and we couldn't. This led to the obvious "explanation": there was something wrong with us.

I had long ago learned not to expose myself to
other people, especially my inner struggles and their
connection to visible problems such as employment
and friendship. It had so often made me a lightning
rod for their good intentions or hostilities. I was
"troubled," or I "needed professional help." It was
puzzling, because I had successfully completed two
degrees, built several teaching studios (groups of
cello students), done good work in my jobs, man-

aged my finances, had an unusually good marriage, and the list went on. Were these people right? While shouldering responsibility for the things that had gone wrong in my life, was I to carry it to an extreme and start heading toward the nearest mental institution? It didn't fit. For years I had accepted that it didn't fit, but no reason was forthcoming. It was one of "life's little mysteries," except that it was a big mystery.

The first clue came with a comment Linda Silverman made at the teachers' conference: she said, "And what about the gifted fitting into society? I've been driven out of academic positions over and over again." I thought, *What do giftedness and problems with employment have to do with each other?*

During the two months between that incident and Annette's test, I thought about this but could make no sense of it. Then at the Gifted Development Center I read an article in *Advanced Development* about gifted people in the workplace:

> Willings (1980) has described the problems that creative adults experience in the workplace. He found that their attitude is not "I'm smarter than everyone else," but, rather, "Why is everyone else so stupid?" The gifted do not understand why the world is so poorly organized and so inefficiently run . . . (Alvarado 1989, 81)

I thought, *Amen.*

The clincher came near the end of Annette's post-test conference. We were winding up the discussion about Ellis, Lewis, and me being in the same IQ range as Annette, proven or not. I said, "You know, this explains a lot. We finally figured out that we can't work for other people. I've always wondered what was wrong with us." Linda said, "And now you know that nothing is wrong. It's actually right—far more than you realized." Shortly thereafter I wrote her this letter:

> It was a momentous discovery to find out that our daughter has an IQ of . . . I am so grateful to you for recommending that we have her tested. We are far more able to serve her needs now.
>
> It has been relatively easy for me to grasp the fact of Annette's IQ, because there has been so much evidence. Far more difficult to process, even just to grasp at all, is the probability that I am as bright as my children. Like most people, I have always equated "genius" with "eminence." I am still trying to fit in my life history with the new picture of me as exceptionally bright. But I don't really doubt it—accepting that I am profoundly gifted has explained just about every problem I've ever had. What a relief!
>
> It is a staggering truth that I could be *that* gifted, but it has resulted in a huge burst of confidence, and a dawning clarity about what I need and what my real work is. The continuing problems of being gifted remain, chief among them being the need to survive in an alien world! But it has made all the difference to know what the basic reality is: my family and I are part of a tiny

minority group about which almost nothing is known or understood. That the general population thinks they understand only makes the problem worse. But just being in possession of the simple facts has created a turning point in my life. It has been indescribably wonderful and liberating to have every recurring life problem I've had, explained: the problem of friendships, of employment, of not fitting in, of being "pathologized" (when I knew nothing was wrong with me!), of being unable to do simple things that other people can do (such as listening to the news), etc. I'll have to leave the list incomplete, or I'll write my whole autobiography.

Near the end of our conference with you and Gretchen, the subject of employment came up, and I commented that I couldn't work for other people without being nearly destroyed by it, and that for years I had wondered what was wrong with me. At that point, I felt a wave of compassion come up out of you, and I knew that I was *home.*

Thank God you have given your life over to the study of giftedness. I really can't begin to convey everything that your passion for the gifted has done for me.

10

THE CRIME WE
DID NOT COMMIT

Along with the immense relief of learning the truth about myself—and not resisting it—came many positive changes to our household. While I was cooking, washing dishes, or even when walking from one room to another, I was always thinking. This even invaded my practicing, which was an annoyance, but I couldn't stop it. There were so many ways in which the decision to have Annette tested had been right. Conversely, had we continued to ignore the issue, or pay minimal attention to it, that would have been a serious error, almost a crime, against our children. I pondered this for many months.

Central to Linda Silverman's thesis is that the gifted are a special needs population. This term has been coined by advocates for those at the other end of the intelligence spectrum, but the words themselves mean "needs that are removed from the norm." This describes the gifted. The farther removed anyone is from the norm, the more differentiated his or her requirements. It was this point that hit me at the teachers' conference. I realized that if we were really facing a situation which was that special, we had better seek advice. I had little respect for experts of any kind, but Linda got around this simply by the things that she said and the way that she was. By the end of those two days, she had hammered it home: early intervention can make a huge difference in the lives of these children.

It did for Annette and Lewis. Before the test, they had two teachers who knew them well, and who had a good intuitive grasp of how to work with them. But we were lacking much specific information. Our formal home schooling efforts predated Annette's test by about two months. We were feeling our way forward, and thought we were doing a good job in spite of many frustrations. These included lack of appropriate curricula, not enough planning time, and a mysterious inability to understand our children as well as we wanted to. Why did Lewis refuse to even attempt something that he thought might be too hard? Why was Annette bored by some things that we thought should interest her? And why did the suspense and conflict in stories scare them both so much? Our response to these things was puzzlement and sometimes irritation.

After the test, although our education about the gifted was just beginning, we already understood our children better, and modified our approach accordingly. To begin with, when Lewis refused to try something new on the cello, I didn't push, I just told him that I thought he could do it. Behind this statement was my absolute conviction that he could. I knew his probable IQ, and I knew that he was capable of far more than either of us could imagine. This created a sense of adventure in me at every practice session: what was going to happen today? I had no idea. I began to invite, rather than require, Lewis to do new things. Where I had nagged before, I now encouraged. When frustrations came, I could navigate through them because I knew that lack of ability was not the problem. Because I believed that there were solutions, I sought and found them.

This had important consequences for my paying students as well. It was my habit to present them with big challenges, to which they often objected. I began saying, "Are you sure it's too hard? Where's your evidence? You can probably do this, and more."

I figured that for every identified profoundly gifted person in the world, there must be five or six, at least, who had no idea of their capabilities. I was sure that some of my students were among them. They were all bright. Many had no trouble grasping the concepts I was trying to put across. Their problems lay much more in the areas of self-confidence and motivation. I knew, for example, that practicing is an activity that is not well understood by many students. Bad practicing impedes their progress, undermines their beliefs in their own abilities, and creates a lot of confusion. In my own students, I could see a low level of confidence or unfocused practicing as a culprit in their playing problems, where they were convinced that they lacked ability.

I started arguing with them, telling them some of what I had learned about "bright people," especially that in some cases the brighter the person the lower the level of confidence. This can happen because gifted people tend not to compare themselves with others' achievements, but to "think of what they know in relation to what there is to know on any given subject, and find themselves lacking." (Silverman 1986, 14)

When I told my students that they were brighter than they thought they were, they argued right back; but I was convinced. Who amongst us can be absolutely certain that we have "topped out" in our efforts? Have we actually realized our full potential, or do we only think that we have?

I asked myself these questions daily. My own cello playing began to change. In the past I had always been crippled by self-doubt, and this is a terrible handicap in any athletic activity. Olympic champions succeed in part because of their ability to focus, to shut out distractions. Surely the biggest of these is that nagging little voice: *You can't do this . . . look there, you missed that one, this is so mediocre, why don't you give up . . . how embarrassing, this is stupid, you're stupid, just give up and try something easier.* Of course this starts up at the very moment you need the best of your accuracy and coordination. When you are in front of an audience, either to delight them for art's sake or to impress them so that they will hire you, this doesn't help. For years I had struggled against this, but now something new was happening. I had always puzzled about my resilience in the face of some disastrous auditions, and about my high level of risk-taking in practicing and performing. The best example of this is my decision to change my bow hold, with minimal guidance, just six weeks before I was scheduled to play a concerto with an orchestra.

When you play a concerto, you are the soloist. You have been recognized as being capable enough to have something of value to share with the audience. You are expected to be great. This requires extensive preparation in the form of months of practicing—the right kind of practicing. During times like this, it is almost impossible to shut out fears related to ego and reputation. To add a major change in technique without adequate time to assimilate it is just reckless. Why increase the already massive pressure on yourself? But I had done this repeatedly, and now began to see the reason: I was more interested in what I was going to learn from any given experience than I was in the outcome. If I played well, fine. If I didn't, I was certainly used to that, but what had I gained that could help me for the next time?

When I saw that my desire to learn everything I could from all possible quarters was the overriding force in my life, I stopped fighting it. And what freedom there was in going with the current instead of struggling against it! I was then facing the opportunity to be rehearsal soloist with the symphony again. This time, the piece was Tchaikovsky's *Rococo Variations*, a technical monster which had always devoured me in the past. But it was also exquisitely beautiful and exciting. I couldn't resist it.

Because of the multiple stimuli and pressures in my life that fall, my practicing was not very focused. I was helped by the fact that the whole issue of confidence had dropped out of sight. Yet my attention was not on my practicing, and in preparing a piece as difficult as the *Rococo Variations*, this can be fatal to the performance. I knew it, but was determined to take advantage of the opportunity before me. I was even nerving myself up to stand in for the soloist in the event of a blizzard—a likely occurrence for that time of the year. Given the poor quality of my preparations, this would have been plain stupid. Luckily, the weather cooperated, and all I had to do was rehearse the piece. I didn't play it perfectly, but that was not as important to me as helping the orchestra get ready for the soloist, and learning what I could by doing it. Plus, I knew it would be fun to play the piece with orchestra, and it was: with that awful little voice silenced, in combination with the tremendous energy release which came from swimming with the current, I could focus on my art as never before.

Along with all these wonderful events came a few trials. One was my search for tutors and mentors. I had begun by calling Charlene Davis, an acquaintance who taught at Casper College, and whom I knew had an interest in the gifted. She agreed to meet with me, and was quite helpful. She became a source of ideas, reading material, and, most important, names of possible tutors and mentors in the community. She could point me to these people a lot faster than I could find them on my own. That the search ended up being worse than looking for the proverbial needle in a haystack was not Charlene's fault.

The problem began with the craziness of Ellis' and my daily life, and the fact that I had a stack of undone chores, to which I added these phone calls. It was weeks before I even got to the first one, and when I finally met face to face with this candidate the results were predictable. He was generous with his books, but as far as the idea of teaching a six-year-old went, even a brilliant one, forget it. I had started in the wrong place, of course—this person did not teach children for a living.

But the point was to find people who were excited about their subject area, dedicated to it, and willing to help a motivated young person. To me, it was a minor concern whether or not they dealt with children on a daily basis.

My efforts were hampered by my reluctance to reveal Annette's IQ, or even to refer to her as being profoundly gifted. All I felt capable of saying was that on the advice of the professionals we had consulted at the Gifted Development Center in Denver, we were looking for someone to work with our gifted daughter. It did not occur to me that I would encounter the same skepticism that all the books warned me of in their chapters on dealing with the resistance of the public schools. But I did. My next and final attempt ended up about the same way. After contacting a candidate by e-mail, I got a referral to another person, along with a suggestion that we enroll Annette in a class offered by one of the local community arts organizations. Again, this person did not understand, but how could she? All I'd really said was that Annette was gifted, added that she was six, and mentioned the Gifted Development Center. I just couldn't tell the details to a total stranger who wasn't all that interested. I felt stymied.

After this second attempt, I said to Ellis, "We are alone in this," and so we felt. We had the responsibility of educating these two phenomenal children, with no community resources in place to help us at all. In our home schooling efforts that winter and spring, as we watched both children leap forward on all fronts, I kept saying to Ellis, "We can't do this alone. They could branch out in several of any given directions, and who knows how far they could go, if only we had a handful of the right sort of people to shoulder some of the teaching load." The problem was not yet the limits of Ellis' and my expertise. He was a math and science whiz, I was good in literature and some branches of the arts, and for a few years at least, we could offer sufficient expertise to the children.

The problem was teacher time, and that to foster their learning, the children needed more *and appropriate* contact with other people. But this was not available, and so we struggled on.

The only other cloud in my life was the awful truth I found in my reading about what a regular classroom does to a profoundly gifted child. I read things like, "In the ordinary elementary school situation children of 140 IQ waste half of their time. Those above 170 IQ waste all their time." (Hollingworth 1942, 299) And, "Many highly gifted children sit in the classroom the way big cats sit in their cages, dull-eyed and silent [because their mental abilities are so far ahead of the material]." (Tolan 1996, 3) Boredom is only part of the picture. If you have thinking processes which are highly complex, and you are constantly presented with material which, to your brain, is oversimplified, and your mind just can't grasp it because you're so far ahead of it, you might begin to doubt your own perceptions. You might get a distorted view of your own abilities. If you are a child, you are defenseless. The teacher, and all adults, know more than you do, so they must be right: there is something wrong with you because you can't accommodate your mind to the material at hand. What appears to be a lack of ability, or a bad attitude, may actually be a fit so poor between that child's mind and the only "education" presented to it, that a kind of death occurs. The killing of curiosity and the unique drives of that individual will most certainly result in a state of apathy and despair which only intensifies with the passing of the years. No wonder so much of the literature on giftedness deals with underachievement and depression in gifted adolescents. At this stage, the damage appears to be irreversible. As I took all this in, I realized that we were sparing Annette and Lewis the harm that had been done to ourselves. As I rejoiced for our children, I grieved for us.

Amazing things had begun to happen in the children's practicing. I would be helping Annette through a problem, and it would suddenly occur to me that she could solve it quite easily with the addition of . . . and three or four more tasks would come to my mind. Solve the problem by adding more to it? Had I not known her IQ, I would have dismissed the impulse. But ever since her test, I had been thinking, and commenting to Ellis, that we had no idea what she and Lewis were capable of. I figured that the most rigorous cello playing tasks I could devise might only scratch the surface.

Annette always reacted the same way to new material that she perceived to be difficult: she would fight it, sometimes to the point of tears, until she saw how to do it. We had to guide, often to prod her over this hump with almost every new idea that gave her problems. It seemed to be part of her learning process. On the uphill side of the hump, we appeared to be stern taskmasters and she a victim of our stiff requirements. At the summit, she would burst into excitement as she saw how to do something and took off with it. This process repeated itself every time I set out to bring her cello playing to a new level. During the climb, especially if she was tearful, I thought, *Seen out of context, this would look really bad to someone who doesn't live here and doesn't want to understand.* I also thought, *If I was her teacher and not her mother, and didn't know her IQ, I'd back off because it appears that this assignment is too tough.* Then the breakthrough would come, she would catch on, and shortly thereafter announce several other important insights related to the main point.

This happened so often that I got used to it for a while and stopped feeling as though I should write everything down so that I would have a record of it later. I didn't have time to write things down, anyway, with Lewis' practicing taking so much of my attention, and Annette coming out of her room every fifteen minutes to tell me her latest practicing discovery. All the while, I was thinking, *Had we not had her tested, both of these children would be languishing for lack of proper stimulation.* Despite their amazing abilities at the ages of four and six, who could have guessed at the actual range of their IQs? Not Ellis and me, and if not us, then nobody else in their lives. I saw that Annette's IQ, and later Lewis' when we had him tested, were the most important items of information we could have about them. With it, we knew that they could probably take any aspect of their learning farther than we could imagine, no matter how hard we tried to infuse our teaching with depth, breadth, and ingenuity. Their abilities were nearly always ahead of our teaching—and we knew their IQs. Had we not known, we might have been deceived by their temporary resistance to challenge. We might have thought the hump was a mountain, and what loving parent would prod a crying child up a slope so steep?

The more I witnessed the results of my teaching them with knowledge of their IQs in hand, the more convinced I was that we had done right. Lewis would sit in front of his music, staring at it, and I would point to the beginning and say, "Okay, here's your tempo," tap a few beats, and he would begin. The first time was often terrible: fuzzy tone, mediocre pitch, off-again-on-again rhythm, to say nothing of his left hand position and bowing. I would stop him, with a reminder that it should sound like the blue la flashcards, and he would play it again, better. Unable to tolerate poor technique, I would correct his bow and left hand, then list all the other things he should be doing: accurate music reading (both rhythm and pitch), good tone, playing in tune, proper cello posture, all while maintaining his good left hand and good bow hold. Just all the things a more advanced player does. Behind these demands lay my knowledge that his abilities and potential were prodigious. Sure enough, sooner or later he would manage everything, sometimes in only two or three attempts. I was often amazed.

Annette's lessons were similar: I would pile on the tasks: read the printed page, keep the good playing habits, then add a new challenge or two, and tell her to do it all. Sometimes she could synthesize it immediately. Sometimes she resisted, but then it would click, in one to five minutes. This went on day after day with both children.

I began complaining to Ellis that we needed a written record of these things, but that I didn't have time to keep a journal. I barely got my household and work-related "to dos" on paper every week; how was I going to manage anything else? But I began to feel like I would burst if I couldn't get some of it written down. So I started tearing myself away from the excitement long enough to scribble a skeleton description of the latest feat. My thoughts grew more and more intense. The children, and I, would have missed out on all of this, had Ellis and I remained ignorant of their actual capabilities. And how many parents had no idea how high their children's IQs might be? It was an easy subject to steer away from in one's own mind, I knew.

That spring, along with the irrepressible need to write down all the things Annette and Lewis did, came the desire to share it with others. I didn't want to tell anyone I knew. Yet I wanted to reach other parents of gifted children.

What were they missing, these families who had the same viewpoint that I had begun with? Who could calculate the loss? The obvious course of action for me was to write a book. I told Ellis that I could feel it pushing at me. He replied, "Well, why don't you write it?" I answered that I had no time, but my strongest objection was that we valued our privacy. As long as we didn't publicize our children's abilities, the press would leave us alone. I said to Ellis, "Do we really want to be in the news? People are just going to have to do without this book." But could I do without writing it? I tried. I told myself that to write a book about my children with the idea that it be published and read smacked of taking your little darlings to Hollywood and selling them to the entertainment industry. I wasn't going to do it.

Then came the day that Annette and Lewis played their first duet. I had prepared them both by making them practice their parts separately, doing everything right. I suggested they try it together, and they got so excited that they could hardly wait for me to arrange their chairs and music stands. I held my breath, as it went almost perfectly the very first time. Then they sent me out of the room, wanting no more help. I ran to find Ellis, and when we returned they were playing it over and over again, sometimes with problems, sometimes not. We each called our respective parent and made them listen over the phone. These children were barely four and six—where were their achievements going to stop? As I wrote of this incident later that day, something in me caved in, and I thought, *People have to know about this. They must be told what can happen when parents and teachers are in possession of all possible information about gifted children. They must be warned of the potential loss created by doing little or nothing.*

The upswing in my energy and happiness that spring brought me to a new high. Despite frustrations, pressures, and setbacks, the mere act of informing ourselves of the children's IQs had brought all of us farther than we could ever have imagined. People needed to know this. The literature on giftedness was saturated with all that goes wrong when gifted children are not served. It amounted to a barrage of bad news, but a story that must be told. How much longer will unidentified geniuses languish in a hostile educational system before we all wake up and collectively decide to do something about it?

Well, here is some good news: when individual parents take the action, spend the money, invest the time, run the risks, and brave the opposition, wonderful things can happen. In our family, we know who we are, and this is the truth that sets us free from all manner of heartache and bewilderment that other gifted people deal with daily. No price can be attached to a treasure of this magnitude.

11

ANSWERS

I now have the opportunity to live the rest of my life based upon the truth about myself. But before Annette's test, I was sapped by the continual drag of all those unanswered questions: Why am I so different? What's wrong with me? Why don't these things happen to other people? And if there's something wrong with me, why do the other parts of my life work so well? This had become a set of nagging symptoms, a malaise for which there was no apparent cure.

One of the most bewildering elements in my life was my effect on certain people. I remember an incident that took place shortly before I started Lewis on the cello. I had just presented my annual public studio recital, at which all of my students had performed, including Annette. It was a great success, and I was relaxed and thoroughly enjoying the social time which followed. One woman complimented me on Annette's playing, and politely asked if I was also going to start Lewis on the cello. I threw my hands up before my face, staggered back a few steps, and exclaimed, "No, no! It's out of the question!" She was put off, and left in a huff. I stood there thinking, *Oh God, I've done it again. Why do I have this effect on people?* There was no answer.

I knew the source of my reaction, and that it had been all out of proportion to this woman's inquiry. She had every right to be offended, or at least puzzled. My problem was that Annette's practicing was already vacuuming up most of my time and energy. I couldn't imagine adding one more thing to my life, certainly not cello lessons for someone under the age of 2½, even if he was my own son. At the same time, I had been fighting my inner sense of his longing to be tall. Thus all of my pent-up feelings produced by this conflict burst out full blast in response to an innocent question.

This was one of the less significant incidents in my long history of clashes with other people. Sometimes I was out of line, and realized it. More often, I was simply being myself—in fact, when I was most faithful to my own deepest needs and drives, other people's reactions were the most extreme.

Probably the most painful incident was the breakup of a seventeen-year friendship, which came about because our respective views of that relationship were so different. I had been experiencing misunderstanding and hurt in my dealings with this person for years. I had even dreamed that she was spitting fiery coals at me. Yet at an earlier stage we had been so close and shared so much, that I was slow to grasp that too much had changed between us. The shift from emotional attachment to a total breakdown in our friendship caused me several years of agonizing. Our conflicts stemmed from one basic source: I needed to examine our mutual problems in an effort to resolve them, and she wanted to carry on as though there was nothing to discuss. To me, this amounted to a pretense in which I could not participate. To her, my need to get to the root of our problems constituted a violation so deep that she could not continue the friendship. In so doing, she revealed her picture of me, and it was devastating.

As I read her final letter, I realized that if I were to accept her view of me, I would have to shrink, slice, and cut myself down until I was smaller than the head of a pin. I knew I had hurt her, and had made a number of mistakes in the relationship. But this letter revealed some things I had never known: that she was afraid of me, and that I had tremendous, long-standing influence and power over her, which I had abused. This was spookily reminiscent of my mother's comments about certain people in her life: "She said she found me intimidating! What on earth could there be about me that anyone would find intimidating?" I knew my mother's self-image, and I knew her. She was not a forbidding or intimidating person. And yet, this was the way that some people reacted to her, and now it was happening to me. We were just normal, ordinary people. In fact, we were the ones who were timid. Why did others react to us this way?

I also encountered this phenomenon while teaching in Wisconsin. After my first four years, both the university and Suzuki teaching loads had grown to the point where the position separated into two jobs. I had run afoul of my university colleagues at that point and decided to stay with the Suzuki teaching. I lasted another three years.

The director of the program, at the time he hired me, expressed admiration for my high level of self-discipline and other accomplishments, but as time passed, the friction between us increased. Near the end of our seven-year working relationship I finally saw to the root of our conflicts. Whenever possible he preferred to speak in euphemism. This drove me crazy because I could never figure out what he was trying to say. He, in turn, was put off by my bluntness. I was also highly organized, and he perceived this as rigidity. It was a personality conflict.

My need to face reality at all costs, to sort out fact from fancy and lay everything out clearly, was a threat so great to him that sometimes he could hardly stand to be in the same room with me. This happened in our final meeting, at which we were discussing an upcoming concert. We were arguing about our students' futures, and the messages we were giving them about adult life. I wanted to showcase a few of the best players as soloists, and he wanted to include everybody in a more typical Suzuki-style concert, which had been the pattern for most of our big recitals. But this performance was different, and he knew it. He knew it by the precedent we had set the previous year, and by prior agreement with our Board of Directors, who had left it to us to sort out the details.

"Look, it's a good thing to reward the best players by choosing them to perform," I finally said. "That's reality. The most qualified person gets the job. If there are fifteen contenders and only one opening, the best person gets the position. That's life, and we shouldn't shield them from it."

He replied in great agitation, "No! That's not true! Everybody can succeed! Life is what you make it!" The air was positively vibrating with negative emotion, and I was open-mouthed as I saw laid bare before me this value conflict which would never be resolved.

Years passed before I saw that this incident was the beginning of my conscious rejection of the Suzuki philosophy. The Suzuki movement is egalitarian to the core. One of Dr. Suzuki's earliest and most quoted maxims was, "All children can develop musical talent." It was dangerously close to, "All children are geniuses." I felt like a misfit at Suzuki conferences and workshops, and always wondered why. Now I know that I was feeling the revulsion of a gifted person against the environment which shouts, Everyone has the same abilities! Everyone should be treated the same way! One educational approach is right for all! Everyone will benefit equally from the same procedures! Nobody deserves special privileges! To recognize superior accomplishment is to discourage others!

Dr. Suzuki himself was not opposed to the showcasing of excellent players. A crucial element in his approach was the one room schoolhouse dynamic wherein beginning and intermediate students learn much from observing the work of the most advanced. I always thought this was one of his more sensible ideas, although hardly original. It was the heavily prescribed pedagogy, the one-size-fits-all curriculum, the rigid steps, which left me feeling that there was no room for deviation either for myself or for my students. Dr. Suzuki and the leaders who emerged from the movement insisted that the Suzuki way was a philosophy, not a method. Teachers were supposedly free to operate within the principles which Suzuki had discovered about early childhood music education. It was true that the Suzuki movement had attracted outstanding teachers and produced some fully competent musicians, even a few prodigies. But the spirit of uniformity was the bedrock of Suzuki's philosophy. From my point of view, it squashed the reality of inborn, superior, divergent ability. Not everyone is a Mozart.

I had met a number of Suzuki teachers who did not slavishly follow Dr. Suzuki's ideology, but many did. Some even bought into his idea that his vision was the solution to all the world's problems: just throw enough beauty at all the pain, evil, and ugliness, and somehow the good will overcome the bad.

My director was not a Suzuki disciple per se, but he was a passionate egalitarian. He and I also disagreed sharply on the way in which musical study should be presented to our young prospective students. He persisted in using the word "easy." I knew he meant that we would make every effort to break down a long, complex process into small steps that anyone could master. But in fact both the individual steps and the entire task required sustained prodigious effort.

Musical study is not for sissies. Every time I heard the word "easy," I cringed. It reminded me of Laura Ingalls Wilder's experience with her editors at Harper and Brothers. She titled one of her books *The Hard Winter* because that was how the survivors of the winter of 1880-81 referred to it. But her editors believed that nothing should be presented to children as being hard. So she had to change the title to *The Long Winter* even though that was not historically accurate. Here it was again, this gigantic pretense among adults, a veritable conspiracy to protect children from reality. It amounted to a lie. I felt this strongly, and my director must have sensed it. I never accused him of dishonesty, but our value conflicts were always in the air. When it all came to a head at that last meeting, I saw that we would never be able to work together.

The Golden Rule did not work for me, and the reason for this was obscure. I wanted honesty and clarity above all else, and this trait which was so deeply a part of me was intolerable to the majority of people I encountered. Some ran away, others attacked. I fared even worse in groups than I did with individuals. Although I was an extrovert I learned the hard way to keep my mouth shut. It was a slow, painful process of building up a shell and learning to hide in it. But I never really mastered this.

Alongside these spectacular failures grew modest success: I was becoming a good cellist and a superb teacher. Many of my students and colleagues liked me. For a time, it appeared that I would have a career in university teaching. Best of all, I got married. During those first years of adjustment, I learned two important things: that Ellis valued truth and clarity as much as I did, and that it was possible for me to become a much better person than I had been when I was single. In the midst of these important lessons, I experienced some of my worst encounters with other people. How could these two realities coexist in my life? It didn't fit. Why was it happening at all?

Near the beginning of my education about the profoundly gifted, I read "Is it a Cheetah?" by Stephanie Tolan. In this article was a list of personality characteristics shared by brilliant people. All items applied, but one hit me in the face: their "insistence on truth and accuracy." This trait above all else had landed me in hot water throughout my life, and yet it was the basis on which my marriage was thriving.

Up until this point I'd had some trouble believing that I might be profoundly gifted. Gifted I could believe; genius seemed absurd. But it fit the facts, and I knew it. To read this was to accept it. A huge release of energy followed, as I relinquished the internal contradictions of a lifetime.

12

THE IRON PROCESS

I have always needed truth and clarity. Despite the serious problems this trait has sometimes caused me, I know better than to try to change it. To perform such radical surgery would be to cut the heart out of my marriage and my life. My long-standing attachment to musical study is an expression of this drive. Unlike my clashes with people, the push for truth has worked entirely in favor of my cello playing and teaching.

At age sixteen I was in the habit of playing string quartets with my sister and two of her friends. My decision to forge a career in music came from one five-second snatch of flawless beauty in the slow movement of a Mozart quartet. I was bathed in cold chills as the utter perfection of that moment flooded my soul. Logic followed excitement. I thought, *We played that measure perfectly. It happened because we were good enough to get it right. We were good enough because we practice our instruments. If I practice more, I will get better.*

Then I can expect more of these moments. Therefore, I need to practice. So I did. It was already my habit to ignore homework. Poor Mr. Rizzi, my honors chemistry teacher, would call on me in class, knowing what to expect. "I'm sorry. I didn't do the assignment last night. I practiced the cello from after supper until bedtime." He would laugh, roll his eyes, and call on someone else.

I dutifully took notes in class, and was able to understand some of the material. But there was always a mysterious chasm between lab activities and lectures. I knew that I was supposed to get the connection, but I never did. Study? Why? I hated school. I had to endure several years of high school academics—in which my English teacher was the only bright spot—before I could focus on music the way I wanted to. I spent those days working at my parents' bookshop after school, and practicing three to five hours per day, seven days a week.

My undergraduate teachers and advisors counseled me to major in music education. From a practical perspective, they were right. I was not a particularly good cellist, therefore I stood little chance of launching any kind of performing career. However, I was not interested in education courses—my passion was performing and practicing. So, despite a barrage of inappropriate advice, I held firm. I was driven. Even my fellow music performance majors noticed it. While in graduate school, I got up early on the coldest of winter mornings to hike over to the music building so that I could fit in two hours of practice before my first class. I often encountered a colleague or two on my way out of the practice room at 8:30 a.m., and they always shook their heads in amazement.

I also remember a conversation with one of my music history professors, during which I mentioned my activities of the previous year: working full time in an office and practicing in the evenings. That had been my life; there was no time for anything else. He replied, "Practicing all evening long, every evening, after working all day? That's amazing. It's . . . Herculean!"

I found this statement to be so surprising that I puzzled about it for years. This professor, although not a performer himself, had a Ph.D in musicology. I would have thought that the rigors he surely had to undergo in graduate school were Herculean, but apparently he did not agree. Even so, in sacrificing nearly all my free time for cello practice, I was only doing what a serious music performance student must do. I knew this, and so did my professors and fellow students, but many of them still acted as though my drives were out of the ordinary.

This pattern continued on into my teaching job in Wisconsin where for a few years I had practice sessions which were of exceptional quality. I remember the day I finally decided to change my technique by direct remedial work. My usual routine included warm-ups, scales, etudes, and difficult passages from the various pieces I was working on. I decided to put all that aside and tackle the problem of speed and fluency. For years I'd been discontented with this aspect of my playing, but had not known how to work on it. That day, I just started experimenting. I began by focusing on physical sensations which signaled that my playing was clumsy and inefficient. This required that I do more stopping than playing, because the longer I worked, the bigger the mess I uncovered. I was determined to be brutally honest with myself:

was my playing as good as it could be? No. The only answer was to analyze my problems, then invent and apply solutions. It was tough and exhausting, but as I began to detect progress I had the sensation of drinking from a cool, pure well. Nothing could have been more satisfying—or more difficult.

Over the following months, my colleagues commented on subtle improvements in my playing, not just in speed but also in tone quality and vibrato. They and other listeners began saying, "Your playing is so natural. You make it look so easy." Me?? The original mass of tight and twisted muscles? I tried to explain the long, sometimes agonizing process I had gone through in college to elevate my playing to the level where I was even in the running for my current teaching position. I tried to explain the recent memorable practice session at which I had begun my remedial efforts. People just shook their heads and said, "Well, you're a natural." But I wasn't. I was a hard worker, and there was a difference.

In discussing the details of that landmark practice session with my colleagues, I noticed that many of them had long ago stopped doing this sort of work, if indeed they ever had done it. One or two of them actually commented, "You're really practicing," as though there were two categories, "practicing" and "really practicing." How had they achieved their levels of proficiency? By merely practicing? Apparently so.

In coming years, I was to create a new category, "perfect practicing," which exceeded all my previous efforts. In perfect practicing I put aside all external pressures, all goals, and when possible all deadlines, and focused on the task of deleting the last iota of flailing from my technique. These practice sessions, which spanned several years, were lessons in self-discipline and personal excellence. It was so much easier to play the cello than it was to make myself stop and work to make it better. But I did so because after one taste from that deep, cool well, I wanted another, and another, and still another. That sense of quenching a long-standing thirst was the fulfillment of my need for truth and clarity. At small cost and much reward, I could slake this thirst simply by practicing right.

Most musicians I knew complained about practicing. They viewed it as a necessary evil, something they had to endure in order to play well. I could tell by the way some of them played that their approach to practicing had not changed in years. Many did not experiment, and I did. They did not all push themselves to higher levels of self-discipline and quality work. They had to force themselves to practice. Although I went through this stage, my practicing had become so exciting that sometimes I couldn't stay away from it.

All musicians are exceptionally motivated people. There is no other way to gain proficiency than through years of concerted effort. At some point I began to deviate from even this high standard. I was so different from the different, so much more driven than the driven—where did I fit?

As if the rigors of cello playing were not enough, during all my undergraduate years I felt the need to write pushing at me. I knew that if I ever changed my mind about majoring in music, I would leap directly into creative writing. But until I completed my Bachelor's degree, the cello took all my energy. Then I landed a job with the Puerto Rico Symphony Orchestra. It was an easy gig; I had time on my hands

and decided to write a book. There were many distractions, among them my own appetite for reading,
playing chamber music, and exploring the island.
Yet every time I got pulled too far off track, I felt a
part of myself dying. I concluded that it was necessary for my sanity that I write; and the more I wrote,
the happier I was.

When I enrolled in graduate school, my schedule got busy, and again I stopped writing—for a few
months. Near the end of Fall Quarter I found myself
sitting in the library trying to write the introduction
to a fifty-item annotated bibliography, the final
project for one of my courses. My topic was cello technique. I thought I could compose a few short paragraphs and be done with it. I had to practice, complete other projects, and study for exams, and
couldn't take the time to do a proper job. That's
what I told myself, but that's not what I did.

Those few paragraphs gave me a lot of trouble.
After about half an hour of struggle, I gave up and
decided that before I could write about cello technique—even briefly—I should define technique. This
proved more difficult to write than I anticipated. An
hour passed and still I was not satisfied. I wrote and
wrote and crossed out and rewrote, losing all sense
of the passage of time. Occasionally I wondered if I
should be practicing, but couldn't tear myself away.

As I worked, I began to notice that the same few
points kept cropping up. I couldn't seem to get rid
of them. Finally I stopped fighting it, and just articu-
lated those few ideas over and over again, trying to
use different words each time. Then I saw that in
this list of ideas I had a set of paragraph topics for my
introduction. I found that I could connect them in
any way that I pleased. The result always flowed. It

was as though each paragraph was a circle, and became a link on a chain. I could rotate each link in any direction and still be able to hook it on to the next one. The more I experimented with this, the more effortless it became, like flying. Suddenly I could see the whole and the parts simultaneously: I could see the overall structure of my introduction, the best way to arrange and connect the paragraphs, where to place every word for maximum punch, and how to bring it all to a conclusion. It was so clear in my head that setting it down on paper was like copying, not inventing. It was some of the best writing I had ever done.

From that day on, my mind functioned differently. A door had opened through which I could see all sorts of new things. It never closed again. Intuitive flashes and large, detailed mental pictures became commonplace. This had an immeasurable effect on my ability to grasp all sorts of things: if I could see it in my mind's eye, I could understand it. This ability to visualize transferred directly to my practice sessions and advanced my cello technique in ways that nothing else could have.

About two weeks after the end of Fall Quarter I was practicing the Fifth Bach Unaccompanied Suite, trying to memorize it for my Master's degree recital which was scheduled for later that school year. Unaccompanied Bach was always hard for me to memorize, the Fifth Suite especially so, because it did not fit the cello comfortably. My usual task sequence for memorizing a piece was: 1) master it technically 2) play it without the music until I knew it by ear and by reflex 3) identify weak spots, and in those passages ask myself note by note, Which finger is next? Which string? Which position (exact spot) on the fingerboard?

Eventually I applied step three to the whole piece, strong and weak parts alike. My goal by performance time was to have every left hand motion mapped out. In this way I'd learned to use my ear, mind, and reflexes together. I could then begin to offset the possibility of those dreadful moments onstage when my mind suddenly went blank, and, God forbid, I had to stop.

That morning I was playing the Prelude with my eyes closed. I'd worked it until I could finally see each move in sequence and on time. Suddenly I could see all four strings. Then I could see several notes ahead. Like street lights coming on at dusk, they began winking at me from their respective locations. This picture was utterly precise, and it grew. Soon I could see a full phrase[1] ahead.

Two major technical problems had suddenly solved themselves: pitch and musical flow. Those little lights showed me exactly where to place my fingers, therefore I played better in tune. The sudden ability to see the coming phrase enabled me to play it without a trace of plodding. It was like driving on a road that had magically become straight, smooth, and familiar.

Several weeks later I was again playing with my eyes closed, and seemingly out of nowhere appeared a picture of the bow, bridge,[2] and strings, all in accurate relationship to each other. Because of this picture I could more precisely position the bow. To

---

[1] The musical equivalent of a sentence.
[2] The bridge is the unvarnished piece of wood, with feet on the bottom and a curve on the top, that holds the strings away from the body of the instrument.

change to an adjacent string, all I had to do was move to where I "saw" it. This was a tiny motion, one I had never been able to judge so well before.

I knew I had made another massive technical leap. I was no longer miscalculating my string crossings, because I had a perfect visual guide. Seeing it in my head was even better than physically looking down at the bridge because looking down at the bridge always caused me to slump forward. But now I could keep track of my bow, maintain good posture, and also see those winking lights that were my new improved road map.

I was amazed the next day when I could again see the strings, bridge, plus not just one, but four images of the bow. Each was in perfect position for playing on its respective string. Seeing these four images of the bow was a step ahead of seeing only one because each was a template into which I could effortlessly fit my physical bow.

I was deeply impressed with the way in which writing had begun to push my cello technique out of the laboriousness in which it had been stuck for so many years. I now lived in a new, freer realm of music-making. I was thrilled with this discovery that writing was as valuable to my cello technique as practicing was.

Despite this knowledge, I could make no more time for writing during that year of graduate work. Practicing and academic courses consumed all of my attention. Then, after completing my Master's degree I settled into the job in Wisconsin. My schedule was full from September through May, but as soon as summer began, I wrote.

I discovered again that I loved writing with a depth and intensity that carried me over all the labors and frustrations that original work entailed. It was odd that my improvement in brain function did not affect my writing the way it did my cello playing. The ability to visualize deserted me when I put pen to paper. My efforts were always so muddled, and I didn't know why. I remember one afternoon when I had been writing for hours and getting nowhere. I thought, *This is really difficult.* Another part of myself replied, *And you like it!* Why was I working so hard, and on my vacation time, too? I couldn't help myself.

Cello playing and writing—and working for other people—comprised the major struggles of that part of my life. Sometime during this period a fairy tale from childhood began drifting through my mind. It was about a princess who had to eat three iron loaves of bread, blunt three iron staves, and wear out three iron pairs of sandals before she could reach her heart's desire. Why did my mind produce this memory? At the time, I had no idea. Now I know that my years of Herculean effort to lift my cello playing and writing out of the mire of mediocrity were a living reflection of this fairy tale. Musical proficiency and fluent writing both required such sustained effort over a period of so many years that I wondered if I would ever enjoy the level of ability that I craved. Working for other people, minus the ability to fit in, required sustained effort of a different kind—punishing and fruitless. It was equally a manifestation of the iron process.

13

WE ARE NOT NORMAL

Near the end of my seven years of teaching in Wisconsin, I took a creative writing course and discovered again the joys of writing fiction. I was in search of fun things to do because I was burning out on the cello. So many artistic compromises came of mixing my love for music with money. However, I had to make a living and was approaching a crisis point in my career. It was time for me to get a doctorate. Then I would be eligible for a tenure track position. I already knew that I was incapable of any more groveling, and where did that leave me? With a nascent writing career? Absolutely not! Writing for money would be as bad or worse than being a professional musician. Prima donnas abounded in every branch of the arts: I'd had enough of such people. Low pay was a fact of my life, and I was sick of it. I had a scary family history of ovarian cancer, and because of this I was forced to think in practical terms: I had to have good health insurance and a regular salary.

My current job also included excellent disability coverage and retirement benefits. This made everything worse. I was driven by the practicalities, and was pulled to the breaking point toward cello and writing.

Ellis and I had been married 2½ years. He had just completed his teacher certification and was job-hunting. Fortunately for me and my crisis, he got a job. I quit mine, we moved, and I looked forward to my life in a nice little house with a white picket fence, children, two dogs, and a cat. I figured that this picture could accommodate my need to play the cello and write.

What happened next was quite different. Although Ellis' brief tenure as a public school science teacher included my dive into perfect practicing, that was the only good thing about this period of our lives. One of our several mysterious employment disasters was brewing.

The job started out fine. It was a small Midwestern school district, and Ellis had four junior high science classes and two high school chemistry classes. His best class, advanced chemistry, had two students. He had an excellent colleague in the classroom next door, and everything appeared to be great.

The problem began with the junior high science curriculum. It was obvious to me that the inventor of this particular educational ideal had no experience with junior high students. The curriculum heavily emphasized hands-on activities and provided for the possibility that every student could pace himself. The science equipment was kept in cabinets to which the students had free access during class hours. Thus, Ellis had to supervise each student separately at whatever stage in the course of study he or she happened to be.

That part wasn't so bad, and with small, well-behaved classes it could have worked. But with the students leaving their seats at different times during the class period to get or return the equipment for that day's work, the opportunities for misbehavior were plentiful.

Ellis' supervising teacher, at the end of his semester of student teaching, had noted approvingly that his approach to discipline was "gentle but firm." Ellis didn't stand for any nonsense, but he didn't bully his students either.

I had a ringside seat, so to speak, at this unfolding disaster. Ellis had a new horror story each day. In a typical incident, he'd be in the midst of helping a serious student, and while his back was turned, two of his worst-behaved boys would be amusing themselves by breaking a faucet at one of the lab stations. His disciplinary measures seemed logical to me, but they didn't work because it was not humanly possible for one adult to supervise twenty-seven thirteen-year-olds, each involved in a separate activity, each allowed by the curriculum to take many trips back and forth to the equipment cabinets. Some of that apparatus was expensive and breakable; Ellis was responsible for all of it. In addition, he had one special education student in that class whom he had to teach without the help of an aide.

He began sending troublemakers to the principal, who would talk to those students, nothing more, then send them back to class. Later that day, he'd say to Ellis, "Why can't you control your classes better?" So Ellis tightened up his rules, including, at one point, making the culprits stand up in a corner, facing the wall.

The principal's comment: "That's the worst thing you can do to a junior high student—humiliate them in front of their peers!"

When Ellis told me this, I said, "If he doesn't like what you're doing, you'd better start sending them back to his office. Let him do his job and deal with these kids."

Ellis replied, "But there's no point in sending them to the office. Nothing significant happens to them. These kids don't even have to pass my class in order to go on to the next grade."

I gasped. "Where's their incentive to learn or to behave?"

"They have none."

I was appalled. I was also worried. Ellis was stuck with that class, that principal, and that curriculum. He was losing weight, and hadn't much to spare. Often he lay awake in the middle of the night trying to figure out how to deal with the problems in his classroom. It was obvious to me that his morale—and his health—were deteriorating.

At Christmas break we had a long talk about it, in which we resolved nothing. Finally I said, knowing how ridiculous the question was, "Can't you just re-sign yourself to being a babysitter?"

"No. I was hired to teach."

How could I dispute that? But it seemed to me that in this situation teaching was impossible. After the holidays I continued to watch him burn out faster than anyone I'd ever known. By mid-January it be-came clear that he and his principal would never be able to agree about what constituted good discipline, and that this conflict was placing Ellis in an unacceptable position. He had indeed been hired to teach, but the conditions of that job required that most of his energy go into classroom discipline.

In February of that year, Ellis broke his contract. He did it with my complete support. His health and sanity were more important than his teaching career. Like me, he had that something deep and powerful within himself that finally stood up and said, *This is wrong. I can't do it any longer, and I won't.*

Off we moved to Casper, where I auditioned for the Principal Cello position with the Symphony. Ellis started his home remodeling business, I got a few cello students, and that is how we limped into the next stage of our lives.

During the packing and moving, on into the following months, I began to ask myself what had gone wrong. I lived with Ellis. I knew him. He was amazing. He could think rings around me. He had the work ethic of a farmer: no stopping for the day until everything was done. It didn't matter to him whether the work was in the kitchen, the garden, or the library; he did it.

His farming background had given him a vast array of practical skills. He could fix machinery. He could make useful and beautiful things out of metal, stone, and wood. He knew how to design, build, wire, plumb, and finish a house. He was a fabulous gardener and cook. I had watched him do some of these things on his family farm in Oklahoma. Most impressive were the incidents in which he had to improvise when the proper tool or part was not available. He almost always found a way to make things work. When dealing with everything from recalcitrant machinery to stubborn animals, his patience and persistence were beyond anything I had ever seen.

His flexibility and encyclopedic knowledge served him well in the classroom. Once, in the physics class that he student-taught, he improvised a demonstration using a doorknob, a piece of string, and a ruler. After this incident, Mark, his supervising teacher, commented, "If more science teachers were like Ellis, we wouldn't need half the fancy equipment we think we have to have."

He also had more integrity than anyone I knew. A few weeks before he broke his contract, we were having yet another fruitless conversation about the students' behavior, the absurd curriculum, and the ineffective administration. My anger at the futility of the situation had been building for months.

I said, "I don't understand why you are still putting so much of yourself into this job. It's impossible for you to teach. It's not even possible for you to babysit. Why are you still trying to give it your best?"

He fixed me with a look and replied, "Would you have me do a shoddy job?"

I had no answer. I knew he was right. It was incomprehensible to me that the administrators in that school district could not recognize the ideal employee when they had one. Aside from Ellis' obvious competence and his willingness to work as hard as was necessary, what single trait could be more valuable than a rock of integrity within someone, a foundation of honesty and a standard of quality so high that nothing could pull it down?

During those months of puzzling that followed our move to Casper, I remembered a conversation with one of my Wisconsin colleagues of several years ago, in which he remarked, "People who teach in the public schools, if they do even a passable job, end up keeping their position and easily getting tenure about ninety-nine percent of the time."

I didn't know whether or not he was right, but he was married to an excellent public school teacher. Presumably he had some idea of what went on. Not for one minute did I believe that public school teaching was easy, but it turned out to be impossible for Ellis.

The more I thought about this, the less sense it made. My bewilderment began to center on how difficult it was for us to make a living. Home remodeling was hardly an ideal starting career for a man in his forties, no matter how healthy he was. We knew it had to be temporary. I watched Ellis' meticulous skills and high standards begin to clash with what clients wished to pay. He would not hurry through a job nor use cheap, substandard materials. Nor would he work for five dollars an hour. All of these factors shrank his market.

We were in the midst of discovering this worrisome fact when I got pregnant with Annette. I had already decided to be a stay-at-home Mom as much as possible, but thought that until she was born I should probably get a day job to supplement my symphony earnings. I mentioned this to Ellis, and added that what I really wanted to do was write and practice. He replied, "Why not? That's probably what you should be doing."

There was my nurturing husband again, encouraging me to invest in my own happiness and creativity. I was always the one who said, "But what about money?" and he always responded, "But what about you?" He had the farmer's optimism, miraculously intact, that dry seasons pass and the crops will grow again if you properly sow the field.

I didn't need much persuading, and so I wrote. I also worried about money. Writing was my hobby, and I didn't think it deserved so much of my time. Why couldn't I stop myself from doing it? During those last quiet months of introspection before Annette was born, I came to see some important things about myself: first, I had to play the cello and write. These pursuits were a necessary condition of my being. Second, I was going to keep doing these things no matter how much financial pressure they caused. Third, I had better stop wasting my energy in the fight between practicality and my creative yearnings. It was time to give in and do my work.

What was this unbreakable attachment to pursuits fascinating, difficult, and beautiful? Ellis had it, too. He would do what was necessary to earn a living (within reason), but his heart was with his own creative work—his personal woodworking projects. So we were united in our commitment to things not practical. We were oddballs. We did not hold the same values as those around us, and couldn't make ourselves over in order to conform. Therefore, it hit like a sledgehammer when I first read in the Gifted Development Center literature that as an unidentified gifted adult, "You may know you are different, but you may not realize why."

I was beginning to make peace with my choice between creative work and money. I didn't know why I was able to do so, and the discovery of my giftedness lay almost six years in the future. My acceptance of Ellis' and my oddness was like a tiny light on my obscure path toward knowing myself.

A small corner of this self-awareness was with me in high school. I was fortunate to have stumbled on it in the form of my pull toward music and writing.

They were my sanity then, as now. The "insistence on truth and accuracy," which caused me no end of pain in my dealings with most people fed me to the bottom of my soul in cello and writing. How would I have fared without them? It's a good thing that I never listened to counselors, teachers, acquaintances, family members, roommates, and friends who told me I was obsessed, impractical, and not well-rounded. It wasn't true. Without cello and writing, I would probably have become depressed and suicidal. No wonder: the iron process with heart's desire at the end is the opposite of the iron process with no end in sight.

In high school, before I settled into music and writing I was just another underachieving, stubborn, argumentative, at-risk kid. And how often are such students mishandled? If the problem in even a small percentage of these cases is unidentified, unserved genius, then the solution ought to be education: first of the general population, then especially of public school teachers and administrators. After this, ignorance can no longer be an excuse, and commitment should follow—public commitment to identifying and serving the profoundly gifted in their earliest years. Then, when they reach high school age, they will be where they belong: in college or already embarked on their life's work.

Does this happen now because every public school district has a legally mandated, properly funded policy for early identification and assessment of the profoundly gifted? No. If it happens at all, it is because parents persevere, with little or no help, in the face of much opposition.

14

SLOW, OR JUST THINKING?

How could a profoundly gifted child fail to be noticed in a regular classroom? Shouldn't his or her grasp of the material be lightning-quick? Such children should be self-identifying, merely by the speed at which they learn. But the truth is that there are many ways in which bright people of any age can appear to be average or even slow.

> Exceptionally gifted children often have difficulty dealing with material other gifted children find easy. The exceptionally gifted see so many possible answers that they are not sure how to respond because no one answer seems to be better than another. For example, Zachery, age 7, with an IQ over 200, was unable to answer the question, "What does a doctor do?" The moderately gifted children answered with any of several acceptable responses and did not find

this a difficult question. Zachery, however, answered that there were so many different kinds of doctors, and they all did different things. Even when encouraged, he was unable to pick one kind of doctor and name something that doctor did. Zachery obviously knew the material but was unable to focus on a simple level . . .

Child D, by age 8, named an amazing 300 shades of color with precise names and assigned them numerical values . . . he originated more accurate scientific names for the entire array of bird species [Hollingworth 1942]. For this boy the concepts of color and birds obviously were much more complex than for the ordinary 8-year-old. Asking D to get a red pencil or to draw a picture of a bird would probably bring a puzzled response where other children simply would carry out the task. Unless one knew D's complex response to colors and birds, one would wonder why he was not complying. (Lovecky 1994, 117)

The more complex and divergent your thought processes, the harder it will be for you to fit in to a society that rewards conformity and shallow thinking. In any classroom where these values predominate, a young profoundly gifted child's best defense may be simply to pretend to be just like everyone else. Or as I did in math, to drift off into speculation that appeared idle but was actually a perfect fit with my own agenda for learning.

All my life I have been fascinated with language.

To me, it is a form of music with all the possibilities for nonverbal expression inherent in its natural rhythm, flow, and beauty. I love words. I love wondering about their shades of meaning, and just like Lewis and his blocks, I love selecting exactly the right word or phrase for the job at hand. So in elementary school, during fractions, I heard the phrase "one divided by five," and off I went into the inner recesses of my mind where I pondered the exact meaning of those words. There are many possibilities: take one piece of paper and cut it five times; the result is six pieces of paper, therefore one divided by five is six. Take one piece of paper and cut it into five pieces; the result is five pieces of paper, therefore one divided by five is five. Take one piece of paper, cut it five times, stacking all the pieces each time you cut so that you are dividing all the paper with every cut. Therefore one divided by five is thirty-two. Nothing in the words "one divided by five" tell you that they mean "divided into five parts, not divided five times," and that the answer is not the same as the result. The result of dividing something into five parts is five separate pieces. The answer the math teachers want is just one of those five pieces. They call it "one fifth." Even now, I have to forcibly remind myself that the right answer is only one of those pieces, one fifth.

Division going the other way is even worse. How about ten divided by five? Take ten pieces of paper. Cut them each five times. Ten divided by five is sixty. Take ten pieces of paper. Cut them each into five pieces. Ten divided by five is fifty. Take ten pieces of paper and divide them into five stacks with an equal number in each stack. Ten divided by five is five stacks. Again, there is nothing in the statement "ten divided by five," to tell you that they do not want you to cut the objects into parts, but to stack them and then to count only one stack, that is, both pieces of paper in the stack: ten divided by five is two.

I never could accept that one answer was better than any other. I eventually learned to grasp the principles and concepts of division, but the language of it bothered me so much that I did not focus well on basic tasks like calculation and drill. I couldn't stop wondering why someone had decided that division meant only a part of the result rather than the result itself. I was doomed. I made it as far as geometry, struggled through algebra, then gave up. I was bad in math, and therefore not bright. This equation, math proficiency equals brilliance, was probably the genesis of my lifelong conviction that I was just an average person.

Another way in which a brilliant person can look slow is in group discussions where everyone else is focusing on the topic, and that person chimes in with a comment that is so far from the center of the discussion that it appears irrelevant. Everyone else looks at you like you're crazy, and you can almost feel them thinking, *Where did that remark come from? That was a silly thing to say.* Meanwhile you are reviewing the long chain of thoughts and associations which led directly from a comment someone made ten minutes ago to what you just said. To you, the connection is perfectly clear. Your first thought is, *Why don't they get it?* Then you realize the futility of trying to explain, particularly since your remark, and you, have been brushed aside, and the discussion is proceeding apace. Then you begin to think, *Why did I open my mouth? I sounded really stupid.* From there it is but a small step to, *Why did I think I had anything to contribute? I'm so slow and inarticulate.* Thus a bright person, especially a divergent thinker, can not only appear stupid to others but actually end up believing it about him or herself. For a child, this experience can be quite damaging.

Such people, by their very brilliance, go against the grain. Their contrast with others may reveal first that they are different and only later that the reason for this difference is extreme intelligence. More often they suffer permanent harm because they end up believing what everyone else is thinking about them instead of what they know to be true about themselves. Put a child like this in a classroom. Is he or she likely to get good grades? Maybe, maybe not. If not, where's the proof of brilliance? The more subtle traits of genius escape most people because so few know what these qualities are and how they manifest themselves when clashing with the outside world. Therefore, it is highly probable that the first encounters between a young profoundly gifted child and his or her school environment will be negative. What are the chances that anyone could thrive under such conditions?

Complex thinkers are also driven to make basic inquiries for which the answers seem obvious. A brilliant person may even ask the same question repeatedly. I did this, and still do, because I want to make sure that I understand; and if there's a deeper or more subtle answer than the one commonly accepted, I want to discover it. This is a great way to look stupid, because the only thing that appears on the surface is the repetition of the question.

I can remember back to college classes and before, raising my hand to ask for clarification of a point which the teacher had already covered, often more than once. The reaction elicited by my questions gave the lie to what those same teachers had said at the beginning of the course, "The only stupid question is the one that doesn't get asked." Not so. Some of them could not believe that anyone would ask such silly questions so many times in one semester.

Unlike my struggle with the language of mathematics, I have reaped immense rewards from asking basic questions. My primal need to understand the deeper implications in the material at hand has left me miraculously unaffected by other people's negative reactions. Still, it has not been fun to bring upon myself the unbelieving, sometimes contemptuous stares and thoughts of others. Nor has it been conducive to a free search for the best way to see and do things. Therefore, a number of years ago I began indulging my habit of asking my silly questions in private.

The most fulfilling manifestation of this process has been in my cello playing and teaching. During one unforgettable practice session, I asked myself, *Why must the fingers of my left hand both curve and spread in order to work properly? What would happen if I never, ever spread them?* The answers are obvious: the fingers must curve so that all four of them can stop the strings (thus changing the pitch), and they must spread in order to be able to reach more than one pitch without moving the hand. If you never, ever spread your fingers, you have to shift your hand every time you need to change notes. What could be more inefficient? I knew this, but decided to explore it anyway. For several days I practiced with my fingers curved but not spread. Of course it went slowly, and I couldn't play any music the way it was written. But I began to experience a new sensation in the knuckles at the base of my fingers: they were absolutely free of strain.

I could also shift all over the cello with greater ease, and had so much vibrato that I had to rein it in. Everything connected with the left hand was far easier, except its most basic function, reaching notes. However, I persevered because my knuckles felt so good. Then, in the midst of a practice session, I had a sudden flash of insight which revealed in perfect detail all that was wrong with the old method and right with the new.

During this time of exploration, I clumped my fingers together in practice but had been forced to play more or less normally in rehearsals. This produced a hybrid which worked better than the old way, but didn't feel nearly as good as the new. I was getting accustomed to the feeling of relaxed knuckles. So, in rehearsals, my hand was busy finding ways to make spaces between the fingers while still preserving that heavenly ease in the knuckles. I was primed for the flash, and in its aftermath was able to perfectly synthesize spread fingers with unstressed knuckles.

I then found that I could zip through passages that had stumped me for years. As every musician knows, this is exhilarating. I remember one afternoon when I was trying the fast passage from the cello solo in Tchaikowsky's *Sleeping Beauty* ballet, which the symphony had just performed. In preparation for the concert I had practiced it with the metronome and forced it up to tempo. Perfect practicing would have been better, but I had a short deadline. It was a hard passage, and I had barely mastered it. That afternoon, I set the metronome at performance tempo and played the passage. It felt so slow that I had to check the metronome several times before I could believe that I was playing it easily at the same speed which had given me such problems only one week earlier. That feeling of slow motion was my signal that I had become much more efficient in my playing. Almost overnight, I had better command of the cello. Thus began my conviction that beginners should start with their fingers close together.

This experience was the musical equivalent of "tessering," a mode of travel invented by Madeline L'Engle in her novel, *A Wrinkle in Time.* Tessering enables you to traverse galaxies simply by bringing two points together: your starting place and your destination. You pull them together, you step across. The amount of time it takes to do this is minuscule compared to the effort you would have expended traveling in a linear fashion. I saw that if I continued to ask myself basic questions about cello technique, I would probably continue to tesser. I did.

My next query was about the bow: Must it be perpendicular to the string? Yes, of course, otherwise it will slip around, and your tone production will suffer. The genesis of this experiment was my students' complaints of wrist discomfort while bowing near the frog (the part of the bow held by the hand). I asked myself, What would happen if comfort for the wrist, rather than tone control, dictated the placement of the bow? I found that putting the bow in a position favorable to the wrist produced an absurd angle. It re-created the same old beginner's problem of the crooked bow. Less advanced string players work hard to overcome this. I thought, *Now what do I do?* and began trying different things. Rather quickly I stumbled on the best tone I had ever produced. It was astonishing. Suddenly there was a center and focus to my sound that had never been there before, and it was so easy to accomplish. I began trying old incorrigible passages, and, sure enough, they were easier. As I took this idea and ran with it, I became convinced that everyone should be approaching their musical studies this way. How much more rewarding it was to tesser than to trudge! I was already becoming a radical, and this experience tipped me over the edge.

Prior to this, I had always maintained that a large part of gaining proficiency on a musical instrument was pure repetition and drill—a component of the iron process. I still saw the truth of this, but now realized that searching for more efficient ways to play was equally productive. Where would I be if I had accepted the prevailing assumptions about spreading the left hand and keeping the bow perpendicular to the string? I would not be the teacher and performer that I am.

It's fun to ask silly questions. This spirit of adventure was with me in childhood, and was still going full strength in junior high. My poor long-suffering Spanish teacher, Miss Smith, had to endure question after question from me about the rules of grammar. I always wanted to know what the answer was behind the answer she'd just given.

Maybe there was a reason I liked to stand in my bedroom with a hand mirror pointed at the mirror on my chest of drawers. There was always another mirror down that long curving hall of reflections.

Now, at the end of a day during which both my children have been arguing with me, and have asked, "But why?" more than a thousand times each, it seems, I look back and feel a certain empathy for Miss Smith. She was patient. When my own children are in this frame of mind, I sometimes want to scream and run away. How can anyone ask so many questions? How can one adult, or two, or three, keep up with that level of inquiry? If it takes a whole village to raise a single child, it takes a universe to bring up a wunderkind. And what happens if the inhabitants of the universe don't agree about the nature of the task? Then parents are left to shoulder it alone.

15

A POPULATION AT RISK

While normal people are living their lives without apparent difficulty, the gifted may be coping, on a daily basis, with struggles that others know nothing about. It is not merely that gifted people may appear slow, unable to follow discussions, or are prone to ask "stupid" questions. Their multiple sensitivities may bring them into conflict with the world in a variety of ways. In my case, before I discovered that I was gifted, I experienced these problems but had no idea what was causing them. My inability to bear the news was a minor difficulty compared with my intolerance for unfairness in the workplace. On top of these moral sensitivities, my emotional responses to the world around me, especially interpersonal relationships, marked me out as being different. I did not understand these dynamics, I only saw that people sometimes drew away from me and acted as if I was not normal. Well, I wasn't.

Probably the most confusing part of my interactions with the world was that my responses were normal for me. When I experienced conflict with other people, the things they said got inside me and stayed there, just like the news. But I could turn off the radio; I could not "tune out" other people so easily. By my late twenties, the number of stinging remarks others had cast at me lay deep inside in a swelling, smarting heap. I didn't know how to cope with this. I figured that life sometimes hurt, but that I could do nothing about it. The possibility did not occur to me that other people might not be as bothered by conflict as I was. Since the idea that I differed from others in this way did not enter my head, I hardly ever talked about it. Thus, the only clues I had came from other people's reactions, which typically added to the confusion.

Among the relatively few positive—or at least neutral—responses I got from others, one was totally puzzling. I had written a short column for one of the Campus Ministry newsletters during my university and Suzuki teaching years. The subject was my struggle with the age-old question, If God is both good and all-powerful, why is the world so full of unchecked evil? It was a highly personal piece. The previous year, my mother had died of cancer at the age of fifty-six. I never could shake my sense of futility about it. To acknowledge that death is a part of life was all very well, but the cancer did such grotesque things to her body; it was so far removed from the ideal picture of someone dying peacefully in her sleep at the age of ninety-nine, never having darkened the door of a hospital or nursing home, that I rebelled against it from the bottom of my soul. In so doing, I rejected God and all things religious.

The column chronicled, in brief, this struggle

and my journey back to God. The pastor decided not to print it, and I knew it was because my writing style did not match the objective tone of his newsletter. He had his own personal tragedies, but they didn't seep into his writing. He apologized to me for not using the piece and said, "I hope you've found the help you need."

I was floored. The entire article was about how I had found the help I needed from God. How could he miss it? Yes, I had been honest about my struggles—that was the only reason I had written about them in the first place. But had that overshadowed my account of the transforming love and hope which had flowed to me from God? This was an absolute mystery, and remained so until I stumbled on the piece a few years ago while trying to make order out of a huge stack of past writing projects. As I read what I had written, I realized that it was nakedly emotional. I actually winced as I saw the depth to which I had exposed my innermost pain. No wonder the pastor hadn't wanted to print it. His was not a publication for raw sores—he was sincere, but bromides were his style.

I was deeply sensitized to my life's experiences, and hadn't even realized how different I was. Coupled with this was an intensity of thought, emotion, speech, and action that other people noticed and commented on. Over the years, it gradually dawned on me that I was an intense person. I perceived this as neither good nor bad, although at times I could tell that it put other people off. It wasn't always good for me, either.

I remember one particularly bad stretch of time, my first year of teaching in Wisconsin, when I had hurt my left hand by playing the cello too much, and playing wrong. I was on a long, downward spiral, and had begun to wonder if my musical career was drawing to an end. I was then in my late twenties. I had been in a state of rising panic all year and at spring break began writing furiously. In a few days I had a bad case of writer's cramp. So I decided to type instead, which only made things worse. I was so agitated that I could feel the stress stabbing at all the muscles of my arms and shoulders. Writing was my emotional outlet; what would I do without it? Music was my joy and my sanity; how could I give it up? I needed to rest my muscles, but could not think in such moderate terms. As I pictured life without either of my creative outlets, I felt more and more panicky, and dug myself deeper and deeper into a hole that I could see no way out of. I could tell that the state of my emotions was part of the problem, but it wasn't like a light bulb I could just switch on and off. Finally the sheer physical pain scared me badly enough that I decided to spend the remainder of my spring break doing nothing. I was depressed.

This was one of my worst tailspins. I had no insight into it for a period of many years, until after the dialog with Betty Maxwell. At the end of that phone conversation, I asked her what would be a good starting point for reading about adult giftedness. She mentioned the subject of emotional intensities as being one of the most important. I thought, *Emotional intensities? That sounds interesting.* A few weeks later I realized that it was indeed familiar.

How many dozens of people had said to me, "Becky, you're so intense about everything. Why do you have to be so intense?" Then a month or two after the dialog, I began to remember all sorts of incidents from my past—times of great joy, deep sorrow, grief, and despair, miserable frustration, and profound happiness. Never before had it occurred to me that all these jagged highs and lows were abnormal. I had no reliable point of reference. Other people's observations varied from acutely perceptive to wildly off the mark. My own interior was normal territory for me. But I was different, even weird, and could tell that many other people thought so, too. "Normal for me" and "part of the norm" were two different things.

When I finally understood this, it was as though I'd been stumbling around in the dark all my life, and suddenly a brilliant light went on. I was, indeed, emotionally intense, and could not change such a fundamental part of myself. I had never really wanted to, but seeing the cause of it and having it so fully accounted for was a source of rich satisfaction. My whole life was beginning to make sense, and what a gift this was! All those mysteries had been a dead weight upon my soul, and I failed to grasp this until they were solved, broken up, and had fallen away like the dust of decades they were, over half of my adult life.

As I continued to learn about the potent combination of sensitivities and intensities among the gifted, I began to pay particular attention to their physical manifestations. I knew that Lewis found certain clothes to be "bugging," and through all my reading discovered how typical this was. I slowly began to get glimmers of insight about myself, and to realize that intense physical sensitivities could be internal as well as external. This accounted for my inability to eat food that didn't seem to trouble other people. I had been aware of this problem for many years. For some reason, I was able to pinpoint a cause and effect relationship between what I ate and how I felt.

Restaurant food had become off limits, unless I was prepared for one or two days of severe fatigue, irritability, and mental fog. Eventually I noticed that I reacted the same way to almost all packaged and processed foods. The culprit? All that was in food that was not food: preservatives, additives, artificial flavorings, colorings, and the like. Others could scoff at the connections I drew between how I felt and what I ate; I had proven it to my own satisfaction. But another discovery lay ahead—I was also sensitive to all manner of airborne pollutants, including things that most people take for granted: perfume, aftershave cologne, scented deodorants, restroom deodorizers, hair spray, new vinyl, and car exhaust. I had heard of "Multiple Chemical Sensitivity" but never dreamed that I suffered from it.

I began to observe my children closely, and noticed that both of them were uncharacteristically irritable, scattered, and cranky following time spent indoors in a public place. Lewis was more affected than Annette, which was in keeping with their differences in temperament. To discover this clash between our health and the physical world was both a relief and a trial. It accounted for my years of severe mood swings and energy ups and downs. It explained why Lewis was a delightful, happy child almost all of the time, but would experience severe lapses in patience and behavior that we couldn't connect with illness, hunger, or fatigue. For obvious reasons, this was difficult. We couldn't so much as go to the library or grocery store without it ruining, or at least damaging the rest of our day.

Imagine that you can't consume the food that

others eat so casually. Imagine that you can't breathe the same air, or rather, you do, but pay a price. Picture a life in which everything comes at you, full blast, all the time—but you have no filters and no shields. This is a physical and emotional reality for many gifted children and adults. It is the consequence of being extremely sensitive and intense, on many levels all at once. Add a third trait of the gifted, unusual perceptiveness, and you have a powerful combination of experiences, for good or bad.

I remember an insight which came to me in graduate school. It did not strike me as being unusual at the time, but I do recall having trouble describing it to anyone else. It was simply that for every human situation, I had observed at least two levels of reality. One was the words people used, the other was their behavior which often belied those words. But it went deeper than merely observing their behavior—it went down into a part of me that, for lack of a better term, I labeled my intuition. With this part of me, I could see that it was the whole person—his or her thoughts, motivations, and actual being—which were at variance. I could not "read" the thoughts and motivations, but could simply tell that they didn't match the words. I took this for granted. It did not seem mysterious to be able to notice these things. I didn't talk about it a lot, because other people were usually so uncomprehending. Besides, it did not increase my trust in people in general. But it did not then function as any sort of life skill, either to protect me from my own judgment when it was poor, or to assist in any other practical way. I only knew it was there.

Years later at that meeting which began the end

of my Suzuki teaching career, I realized that not only could I sometimes tell what others were feeling, I could literally feel what they were feeling. This was a major jump in self-understanding, but I had no idea that it had any connection with giftedness until after the children's IQ tests. In *Counseling the Gifted and Talented,* edited by Linda Silverman, I read:

> Sensitive and compassionate gifted children . . . seem not only to know what others feel, but to actually feel the feelings within themselves. This is particularly true of intense and negative feelings. Whereas most children know when a parent is angry, sensitive gifted children feel the anger inside themselves . . .
>
> Children who feel the feelings of others and are unable to set interpersonal boundaries may feel too much pain coming from other people . . . (Lovecky 1993a, 39)

To gifted children or adults who experience the emotions of others within themselves, simply being in a room full of people can be unnerving. How could you sort out your own feelings from the mix that is in the air, and also in you? And for the profoundly gifted, these three traits, sensitivity, intensity, and perceptiveness, are tuned to an unusually fine pitch.

What does this mean for profoundly gifted children? A typical school probably contains the following airborne pollutants: perfume, aftershave, scented deodorants, fumes from cleaning fluids, marking pens, and art supplies. Add to this a cafeteria lunch which is almost certainly not free of additives, preservatives, artificial flavorings, and colors. A profoundly gifted child who has sensitivities of various kinds, recognized or not, will be severely affected. Combine this with perceptiveness and a state of emotional intensity. If such a child is in a regular classroom, unidentified and unserved, the following conditions are likely: he or she is recognized as being different, but not necessarily capable. Maybe the other children react negatively to this, whether openly or not. This gifted child can feel their hostility. He or she can also most certainly feel the teacher's feelings. Maybe they all wish that this child was not in the class. Maybe this child has extreme reactions to all kinds of situations, both because of emotional intensities and a body chemistry which is totally out of balance. Virtually everyone in this child's school environment could be thinking, *What's wrong with Susie? I wish she'd go away. Why doesn't she just shut up?*

How is Susie going to feel about herself under these conditions? How would you feel if you were bombarded with thoughts and feelings that you could not screen out, that were all about you being weird and troubled? How could you know that these were others' feelings about you, and not your own? How could you know that your inability to control yourself, especially your emotions, came from a potent mix of chemical imbalances, your own sensitivities and intensities, plus low level chronic depression brought on by a severe case of intellectual starvation? You couldn't know.

The younger you are, the harder it is. And if your parents know little or nothing about giftedness, they do not know about your special needs. You are literally stuck in school to cope with a terrible mix of physical, emotional, and mental stresses, five days a week, nine months a year. How could you possibly emerge from twelve years of this with a great self-image and a zeal for learning? If you are especially creative and divergent in your thinking, you have begun to learn that the world does not treasure these qualities in the raw. It may take you years to come to believe in the value of your own unique abilities. How much of your life will then remain in which to fulfill your destiny—to give to the world that important discovery or contribution that your mind, and maybe yours alone, is capable of?

Picture today's world bereft of the legacy of a Thomas Edison, a Benjamin Franklin, or a Henry Ford. Or, if you think technology is a mixed blessing, choose a contribution that is less debatable. Consider the life of Joseph Lister, pioneer of antiseptics in surgery. His battle for recognition took most of his life. Had he been without nurture in childhood, and without a mentor for much of his career, would he have had the necessary independence of thought, confidence, and opportunity to develop and prove his important theories about bacterial infection? In your imagination, delete the effects of his work from our modern world. People would still be dying of post-surgical gangrene. We would still be in the dark ages in that area of medicine. It is all very well to say that sooner or later some other gifted person would have discovered the same thing, but what if Joseph Lister saved your great-great-great grandmother's life? Would you have liked him to get the nurture and care his young mind needed?

Now fast-forward to the present. Have the persons destined to find the cure for cancer been thwarted early in their lives because of a national case of shortsightedness about who our most gifted young people are and what they need? We have been apathetic for too long. Our mothers, sisters, uncles, aunts, fathers, and cousins are dying of cancer. Let us seek out and serve the coming generation of the profoundly gifted, so that we ourselves can reap the rewards of their work. A free and appropriate education for all must include our most brilliant students and their special needs. Such measures are not a privilege, rather, they are an act of prevention that could serve every man, woman, and child on this planet.

16

THE SELF

During much of my adult life I have done battle with a large and important part of me that always seems to win, against my own better judgment. After the conflict has been resolved, I look back and realize that it was a good thing that I lost.

The most striking manifestation of this phenomenon came a few years ago, in the wake of a concert. I had played the Saint-Saens Cello Concerto with the Wyoming Symphony Orchestra, my first solo performance in more than a decade. I played from memory. Annette and Lewis were five and three years old, and I had an average of one hour per day of practice time. In order to prepare, I had to put myself in a practicing prison, where I devised an ironclad routine which omitted nothing. This ensured that there would be as few holes as possible in the finished product. One of the most nerve-racking aspects of this experience was that I had only one chance to do it right, because there was only one performance. This was the reality because I was not a world-class soloist.

Not only was I not a world-class soloist, I had a terrible inferiority complex. My months of preparation for the Saint-Saens performance predated the children's IQ tests by about a year. With so little self-confidence, I could picture all sorts of meltdowns on stage. It was motivating. Day after day, week after week, month after month, I forced myself to focus, to concentrate, to drill and work and drill again. I was relentless.

The performance went well, and afterwards I gave myself a little practicing vacation. I did not touch the cello for almost a week. Then, when I resumed practicing, I did not work very hard. I played, but did not attempt to capture my mind. Consequently, it wandered. This was fine with me, because my only goal at that time was to keep my muscles and re-flexes in shape. After a few weeks of this delicious leisure, I decided it was time to get back to work. So I began trying to focus my mind. I could not. I tried harder. Nothing happened. In the space of a few short weeks, it appeared that my brains had turned to mush. Day after day I tried and failed to pay atten-tion to what I was doing while I sat behind the cello. It was hopeless. All during this time I was teaching, and delivering the usual lectures about Paying At-tention To What You Are Doing While Practicing.

Meanwhile I would be thinking, *What's the matter with you? You can't even accomplish what you are telling them to do.* It was intensely frustrating, and the longer it went on the worse it got.

I kept saying to Ellis, "I've lost my ability to focus! I took three weeks off from quality practicing after the concerto and it's destroyed the good habits of a lifetime! This can't be happening."

He usually replied, "You need to write," or "You need a break from your routine," or "You need exercise and time to yourself." He was probably right, but none of these things was available in sufficient quantity. So I labored on.

The performance had been in April, and the end of August was approaching. I began to despair of ever getting my mind to cooperate again. What had become of perfect practicing, that ability to focus on the tiniest details, sometimes for weeks at a stretch? It was gone. The irony of it was that my manuscript on practicing was all about how to focus the mind and reap the resulting benefits. I wasn't finished writing the book, but what in the world would I have to say about the subject now? I was incompetent. It seemed that the more I tried to capture my attention, the worse it got.

One day I said to Ellis, "This is impossible."

He responded, "Why don't you just let your mind wander? Why fight it?"

This was a new idea. I decided to try it, out of pure desperation. Not for one minute did I believe that it would really work.

I don't remember the time lapse between my first attempt at letting my mind wander and the next important practicing discovery, but it was not long. When the revelation came, it was the best yet. I always knew when I had happened on a great idea, because it was another case of tessering: a sudden, huge leap, after which I could play faster, louder, with better tone, more finesse, increased control in slow passages, more of a sense of spontaneity and play, all with a new level of ease. This was so compelling that I couldn't drag my mind away from it. It was beautiful in its logic and simplicity.

In the space of a few days, I had gone from being unable to focus my mind to being absolutely fixed on one idea. This state of excitement and concentration lasted for several months. As I pondered this series of events, I found myself remembering a section from *Cradles of Eminence*, by Victor and Mildred George Goertzel, which I had read a few years ago. This book depicts the formative years of selected famous people.

At my first reading I had noticed a number of similarities between the home environment we were providing for our children, and some of those described in the book. Economic prosperity was not necessarily a common factor; parental attention and sacrifice seemed to loom much larger. But I was now recalling the book's conclusion, where the authors summed up all of the various circumstances the majority of their subjects had in common. In the discussion about important discoveries, they pointed out that intuitive leaps or solutions to big problems had often come during or at the end of a period of unstructured activity. Sometimes it was a year or more off from formal schooling, sometimes a walk in the woods during an extended vacation. The authors theorized that this lack of structure was a prerequisite for the resulting discoveries. I had agreed at the time, but now I was really convinced.

In retrospect, what could make more sense than the process my mind had gone through during the previous year? First a long period of rigorous work— a tight structure, maybe too tight. Then, a release, followed by a huge jump. I had not understood this process at the time, and had therefore fought it. I had no concept that a mental "walk in the woods" could be of such immense help to my work. I had known the value of time off, but this was a new slant on it: to me, a vacation had always meant no practicing, not no paying attention while I was practicing. Because of perfect practicing I was a much better cellist, but I didn't have the wisdom to see that it was time to break out of my own mold.

Ellis had topped me in the matter of asking silly questions. I had made any number of absurd inquiries about cello technique, but none about the process of practicing. What could be more ridiculous than asking, Why should you pay attention to what you are doing while practicing? The answer could not be more obvious: you need to know your goals, and to implement them. To gain musical proficiency you must form good playing habits, and this demands close attention. Learning to focus the mind is one of the first battles beginners fight. In few other educational activities is prolonged, absolute attention even a possibility. With a musical instrument in your hands, the number of tasks, and their level of detail, can be almost infinite. This is true if you really want to do it well.

Many musicians never reach the level of sustained concentration in their practicing that they should, but I had to, because it was a case of the tortoise and the hare. Others seemed to possess a mysterious early command of the cello that I longed for but did not have. To even approach it, I had to submit to the iron process.

In the aftermath of this failed struggle to trap myself in my own good habits, it occurred to me that I had witnessed an important new event: the need of the mind to breathe. On the "inhale," when air travels a narrow path through the bronchial tubes and into the lungs, I had channeled my attention into just a few selected areas. I had severely restricted it, and not allowed it to stray. On the "exhale," when carbon dioxide leaves the body and diffuses out into the air, my thoughts also had to expel themselves from the limitations I had placed on them for so long, and wander out into the "air" in my head. Airheaded practicing just about describes what I thought I did that year from April through August. But the result was anything but vacuous.

This new theory about the mind needing to breathe fit very well with my past habits of perfect practicing. But I was still trying to inhale when it was time to exhale. This was because I didn't know the needs of my own "body," and was trying to proceed on information about myself that was entirely wrong and contrary to nature. After the concerto performance, a very deep, wise part of me knew what I needed to do, and just went ahead and did it.

This was my biggest battle, but not the only one. It was this part of me that always asserted itself right after I had clamped down extra hard, telling myself, *I've got to be more frugal* . . . Then I would go buy a new outfit. *I've got to work harder* . . . Then I would find myself at the library checking out a Mary Stewart novel. *I'm going to stay with this cello teacher one more year (even though I'm not learning anything) because I'm almost done with my degree* . . . And then I took steps to transfer to another school. *I'm going to stay in this artistically deadening job a few more years because the money is so good* . . . And then after the first year, I moved, jobless, to a new, large city, expressly for the cultural benefits to me as a lifelong student of the cello. *I've got to get a day job so that we have some extra money before the baby is born* . . . but in my heart I knew I should write, and that is what I did.

I gazed back upon all these lost battles and decided that maybe it was time to pay attention to this phenomenon. My airheaded practicing had just come to an end. I was skipping and leaping around the cello and in my spirits as well. I had met Linda Silverman at the teachers' conference about a month earlier, and we were soon to have Annette tested.

Sometime that year, I read about the "Self." I gathered that the Self is a deep, hidden part of us that is of primal importance. I am neither a psychologist nor an expert in this subject, but I do know that what I read fit with what I had learned. The Self is often ignored, discounted, squelched, or even annihilated. If the needs of a particular Self differ from the norm, and nobody realizes it, that Self will be damaged. This describes the problem that many gifted people have, and that I had for so long. First, I did not know that I was gifted. Second, I did not even suspect that I was profoundly gifted. And third, I knew—but ignored the knowledge—that a deep and important part of me sat in the driver's seat and steered my life, in spite of the contrary instructions I tried to issue from the passenger's side.

Once I realized that it was my Self, the Self of a profoundly gifted adult, and that this Self would be in charge with or without a fight, I set a goal to heal this lifelong split. I began to listen to my Self, to think about it, and to honor its needs.

This decision was of greater benefit to Ellis and the children than any other single gift I could have devised. As I learned more about the characteristics of gifted people, I saw all these traits, but in differing combinations, in Ellis, Annette, and Lewis. My attempts to know and honor my Self grew into a commitment to know and honor these other three distinct and separate Selves with whom I lived.

I had always known that Ellis had a different personality type than I. He was calm, I was excitable. He was quiet, I was talkative. He was restrained, I was impulsive. I had observed that these differences also permeated our work styles. His way of solving problems, organizing his time, and dealing with clutter were often opposite to mine. Since I thought I was the organized one, this created conflict, especially after we started our algae distributorship and began working together at home more. It was a big load off Ellis when I stopped badgering him about how he used his time and how he handled problems.

I was organized, but in the way that suited my style. After I decided to honor my Self, and pay attention to his, I began by simply observing him and theorizing that he could accomplish more if I would just let him work in the way that suited his style, according to the dictates of his very different Self. The results were gratifying. We have both become happier and more productive. I waste much less of our collective energy on issues of control and dominance. We cooperate. We are creating synergy in our relationship, our family life, and our work. Best of all, I have quit saying to Ellis, "You're the smart one, you solve this problem!"

17

TAKING CARE OF OUR SELVES

From the moment Annette was born we were overwhelmed, just like all new parents. Years before I got married, one of my friends who had recently had her second child commented to me, "There's no such thing as an easy baby."

I hadn't a clue what she meant until I found myself creeping through postpartum, snatching sleep in half-hour installments, gobbling cold meals, all the while watching our house degenerate into unprecedented chaos.

After life had settled back into something resembling a routine, veteran parents began saying to us, "It doesn't get any easier; it only changes."

I thought, *Of course it gets easier. How could anything be harder than breastfeeding?*

After Lewis' birth I discovered one thing that was harder: breastfeeding a wide-awake newborn while raising a toddler. I was thirty-eight. By the time Lewis weaned himself at thirteen months, I couldn't tell if things had become easier, because I was too busy to think about it. I suspected that those veteran parents were right.

As Ellis and I staggered out of the unremitting fatigue of becoming parents at middle age, we ran straight into the demands of home schooling Annette and Lewis. Then we began to realize that, difficult as it was to meet their prodigious needs, an even harder task awaited us: taking care of ourselves beyond the point of merely getting enough rest and eating our meals on time. During the early years, we were so sleepy and overworked that for a time we almost lost sight of our own creative drives. Our health, and that of the children, had to come first.

Our first flicker of reawakening our own creative activities came with a habit we formed after Lewis was born: giving each other "no money" gifts. One year I gave Ellis an entire month off from dishwashing. Sometimes he gave me a year's worth of weekly foot massages. The best present he ever gave me was one hour of morning writing time per week, subtracted from his work time, when Lewis was just one year old.

From that one weekly hour blossomed the first draft of my book on cello practicing. After the gift expired I still found myself snatching an hour of writing here and there, often at the expense of my practicing. I was blissfully happy to be writing again, but it was almost impossible to sustain both writing and practicing when I had to keep my cello playing in shape for my job with the Wyoming Symphony Orchestra. Gradually I stopped writing. The death knell was Lewis' early start on the cello before the age of 2½.

Just about the time both Ellis and I had begun to

feel that the requirements of daily life were devouring us whole, we discovered the blue green algae. We had heard about it. We had read about it. But nothing could compare with trying it, and until we did so we had no idea what we were missing. Overnight, our awareness changed, both about our own health and about our options for making a living. We were amazed at the quality of the algae and what it did for our bodies. So amazed that I, for one, could not stop talking about it. Once we realized that we could become Cell Tech distributors, we plunged into the business. It was fun, plus in the following year we gained more knowledge about alternative health and nutrition than we ever dreamed existed. We also caught the excitement of the New American Dream: making a living from home, being our own bosses, and tailoring our work schedule to the demands of child raising and, in our case, home schooling.

Before we started the algae business, Ellis was gone all day. His hours were long, the work was hard, and he had to do bookwork almost every evening. He was in his late forties. It was not a sustainable combination. We decided that he should phase out the remodeling business as quickly as possible.

During the early part of this transition, life was a whirlwind. I worked every evening and weekend, calling potential customers, mailing out information, writing promotional letters—anything and everything we could think of. I found a source of energy within myself that I didn't even know existed. Occasionally I thought about writing, but the algae business was so obviously more important that I wanted to put all of my spare time and energy into it.

We expected our new efforts to produce a living

for us in a matter of a year or two. It didn't happen that quickly. This was a terrible blow to me, but I finally accepted the slower pace at which our business was going to grow. I discovered a new level of tenacity and resilience within myself that even many failed auditions had not revealed.

During the next two years we juggled my symphony job, my teaching studio, the algae business and—of necessity—Ellis' remodeling business, now part-time. He too spent every scrap of his spare time on our algae distributorship. We crept forward, but at a cost.

One day Ellis said to me, "I have no heart."

I was tempted to laugh, because "heartless" was the last adjective anyone would use to describe Ellis. But of course he meant that he was losing heart. It didn't help that I had recently resumed writing, this time robbing my algae work time. I thought I shouldn't do so, but the push of my Self to communicate with other parents of gifted children had become even stronger than my drive to get the algae business launched. I didn't realize how much stress this placed on Ellis until he said, "I have no heart."

He then told me that he was haunted by visions of beautiful wooden bowls, vases, and desk clocks, all of which he was fully capable of making, if only he had more time and the right tools.

We'd had The Tool Conversation many times. Before I married Ellis, I didn't know a router from a table saw. Even after discussing many tool purchases, I still had to ask the same questions.

"What is this thing you need?"

"A lathe."

"Oh yes, I remember. And tell me again, what does a lathe do?"

"It makes it possible for me to turn round things like table legs—and bowls."

"So you could make us some furniture if you had a lathe?"

"Sure."

"But what you really want to do is make bowls and vases and stuff like that, right?"

"Right."

"But don't you have a lathe already?"

"Yes, but it's that little mini-lathe, remember? If you want doll furniture or small bowls, it would work okay, but . . ."

"But what?" I asked.

His facial expression appeared right on cue: stress combined with a sort of painful patience. "But it's not a very good lathe."

"Oh. How much does a good one cost?"

"I'll go look it up." Off dashed my easygoing husband, like Lewis on the trail of a puzzle piece. Back he came, tool catalog in hand. "This one costs five thousand dollars."

I gulped. So many times I'd observed the reaction of non-musicians upon hearing the price of a fine cello or bow. They all exclaimed, "That much money for a fancy piece of wood?" or some such other expression of shock. So I said nothing. I knew that to pay less for a poor quality lathe would be more expensive in the long run than to buy a good one to begin with. At this point in The Tool Conversation I became a marshmallow.

"Well, if you're going to buy yet another tool, it had better be the absolute best you can find."

"I agree."

"Can we afford it?"

"We'll find a way."

We always did. When Ellis needed a tool, my chronic concerns about money were always mysteriously transformed into solicitude for him. After this latest conversation, I wanted him to have a lathe. Then, when I realized he needed woodturning time, I wanted him to have that also. I could see that we'd been starving his Self, and must not continue to do so.

"Well, how are we going to make turning time for you this week?"

"I don't know. What about your writing time?"

"You know I should be spending more time on the algae business, not less!"

"Yes, but you have to get this book written."

"I know, but if I spend time on a book that may or may not get published, when we really need the income from the algae business, where will we be?"

"Where will you be if you try to suppress this book?"

"Where will you be if you end up without turning time?"

"Heartless."

"Right."

We circled around like this for several years before crafting a household routine that worked. Each daily choice was a gamble: if we subtracted too much time from making a living, we endangered our finances. If we did not feed our creative needs, we drained ourselves. Then we lost heart. If we did not take proper care of the children, they lost heart.

This situation required a balancing act such as I had never before achieved. We had to plan each week down to the tiniest detail. Who was going to teach the children, and when? How would the bread get baked? When did we fit in the errands? My cello teaching hours were set, but I needed planning time, plus I had to practice. If Ellis had a remodeling job, we had to sacrifice his turning and my writing. We protected our scheduled home schooling hours as best we could and stuffed in algae work whenever possible. Late nights, early mornings, and overloaded weekends were part of the routine.

By this time I had fully accepted our oddness. Other couples might ask each other over supper, "How are we going to make ends meet this month?" But I doubted that they followed this question with a detailed discussion centered on how much time they should gamble on heartlessness prevention. It seemed obvious to me that our wild departure from the norm centered on our commitment to the needs of our Selves and our resulting inability to pursue money. "How can we keep our sanity?" overtook "How can we earn a living?" I knew full well that most other people did not live their lives on that basis, and with good reason.

I was acutely aware of the financial hazards that we created by spending so much of our time on activities that didn't guarantee us a regular paycheck. In spite of my creative urges, without Ellis' constant encouragement I would never have gambled so much of my time on writing; it seemed a financial dead-end. By contrast, his woodturnings could and did sell. People picked up his desk clocks and gasped. Often they gasped at the price tag as well, but Ellis came to expect that. He knew he was a fine artisan, on his way to becoming an artist, and he wasn't going to work for pennies.

As with our algae distributorship, Ellis' woodturning did not generate a significant amount of money overnight. But as I watched him grow happier and more relaxed, I saw that his turning was no mere luxury. It fed him the way writing fed me. Best of all, we were setting a fine example for Annette and Lewis. Although teaching them demanded so much of our energy, we'd succeeded in reserving some time and heart for ourselves. We were also pursuing work that we loved, and raising them with the message, You can and should find paying work that you enjoy. We'd turned our backs forever on that heartless requirement: You MUST stay in a job even if you hate it.

Therefore, money was a problem, and likely to remain so until one or all of our several new careers began producing sufficient income. Meanwhile, we were happy and so were the children. It took a blend of courage, instinct, organization, and sheer recklessness. As such, it was a stupendous feat, and entirely worthwhile.

18

HELP AT LAST

We had Annette tested in November of 1998. Since then, many things have improved at our house, especially our understanding of our children. Although we daily face the puzzle of raising two small people whose minds are years ahead of their bodies, our commitment to know and serve them has made our task much easier.

Lewis is a divergent thinker. I read about him in *Counseling the Gifted and Talented*. One of the most helpful passages stated,

> Children who are divergent thinkers find it hard to organize thoughts, feelings, and materials, both at home and at school. Although it is somewhat acceptable for adults to be absentminded, it is not acceptable for schoolchildren. For highly divergent thinkers, however, many adult organizational schemata seem alien. The standards adults use

to organize schoolwork are frequently based
on a linear format that gives divergent thinkers difficulty. They see problems as wholes,
and dividing them up into what appear to
be arbitrary parts does not seem reasonable
to them; in fact, they cannot think this way
at all. In addition, decision-making and setting priorities are difficult because all the
thoughts and feelings of the divergent
thinker are interconnected; thoughts and
feelings all seem to be equally interesting
and important. Finding a starting point is
impossible for the child. (Lovecky 1993b,
32)

I now know better than to simply order Lewis to
clean up his desk. He will need to learn from us how
to organize his living space and his time, but in a way
that does not interfere with the drives of his Self.

Coming to know my own Self, to befriend it and
learn to pull in tandem with it has been of tremendous help to Lewis, because I have exerted the same
efforts on his behalf. His drive to think, to express himself, and to try to do everything in as many new and
different ways as possible, is primary. We gain nothing
by trying to oppose it. The main challenge of Lewis'
life is for him to learn to manage his extraordinary level
of intelligence and still be able to cope with daily living. This is a big job for someone who would rather
think and experiment than do anything else.

I have known from the very beginning that Lewis
would not do well in school. Like many gifted people,
he would rather set his own agenda for learning, and
this agenda does not fit the norm. Even here at home,
we had difficulty honoring his unique and overpow-

ering drives until we began to understand their source and nature.

At the conference following Lewis' IQ test, Linda Silverman said, "Continue to follow his lead in the home schooling." It was a big relief to hear this. It confirmed our sense that we should make way for his inner imperatives. At this stage in my education about the profoundly gifted, I had finally dumped the idea that children cannot be trusted to direct their own learning. I saw so much motivation in my own household, and knew that it sprang from the creative push of the Self. I knew Lewis would learn those things which were most important for him. Along the way, we would also be able to teach him the other things he needed to know, in short, to give him a well-rounded education.

The main consequence of Ellis' and my getting to know Lewis is that his life in this house is much easier than it used to be. We have a lot more patience with his tendency to get lost inside his own head—we understand that it is a vast, intricate place with numerous byways that are constantly calling out to be explored. Every answer leads to a new question. Each mathematical insight leads to another. All the little songs have to come out.

In the midst of this, we have managed to teach Lewis that it is a necessity to focus his mind on tasks like eating, dressing, and brushing his teeth. We have learned, by a combination of instinct and experience, that the more freedom we allow him for thinking, the more able he is to focus on all manner of mundane but essential activities.

Not long after I discovered that my mind needed to breathe, I realized that his probably did too. By allowing him time in which to "walk in the woods," we have helped him to balance his daily life. Considering the magnitude of our early problems with getting him to remember what he was sent into another part of the house to do, this is a major accomplishment.

During his cello practicing I still face many unanswered questions. While he's warming up and I see his face go blank, where is his mind? Obviously not on the cello, yet is that a good reason to stop him and remind him to pay attention? Maybe his mind is wandering off toward an important musical discovery; do I dare to interrupt? Is he engaging in productive or non-productive woolgathering, and how do I tell the difference?

After a few minutes I stop him because I am compelled to correct his bow hold and sitting position. I remind him to pay attention, then he starts again. I think, *Maybe it was wrong to tell him to focus on what he's doing. How do I know what his mind needs? I have no idea where he's headed; does he?* Where's the teacher's manual for a child with this type of intelligence? Lewis needs leeway in his practicing. I try to provide as much freedom as possible without sacrificing the structure and guidance that he surely needs. But how much of it does he need? I have no answer except that which I try to puzzle out each day while helping him with his practicing.

It has been important to learn Lewis' IQ, but it has been crucial to learn about all the other personality traits surrounding it. Without this information about the whole gifted person, our relationship with Lewis might have degenerated into a hopeless power struggle. Every parent knows how easy it is to fall into negative patterns with a child when there are incorrigible problems whose cause is obscure. I thank God for the education that Ellis and I have acquired as a result of our readiness to believe that our children had special needs and would benefit from early assessment and intervention.

Unlike Lewis, Annette appears to have been an easy child to raise, so far. She is organized, focused, and goal-oriented. She is a good test-taker, and would probably be considered academically talented. Her temperament is as intense as Lewis' but she is able to manage it differently. She is a lot like Ellis. Over the years, I have watched him in awe, because he is not overwhelmed by his emotions. *How does he do it?* I used to ask myself, *Why can't you be like that?* But I don't do that anymore. It is as wrong for me to try to stamp myself with his image as it was for me to interfere with his Self. All the same, I envy Ellis and Annette, because perhaps they will not be told they are troubled, just because they can't keep their emotions under cover. They can, and this certainly helps in daily life.

But we face subtle challenges in raising and educating Annette. These problems are hard to identify, and only appear as we attempt to lead her to the outer limits of her abilities. The difficulties connected with her rapid musical progress and her early need for independent practicing could fill several volumes. Just because she wanted to practice alone, and was motivated enough to do so, did not mean that she had good practice habits at the age of 5½.

It is my job to help her learn these skills, but what am I to do with a student whose lessons are two to three hours long, because she is ready for in-depth discussions about the finer points of tone production? How do I find the time to check the accuracy of her etudes, scales, and pieces? It's a scramble. No

time is left in which to give advice about how to practice—what to listen for while learning a new etude,
how to memorize the fingerboard, and how to culti-
vate speed without sacrificing accuracy. She will need
to learn all of these things, and she is slowly absorbing them, but this is not the focus of our lessons.

The faster the pace of her development, the
harder it has been to achieve depth. Cellists must
learn to read music in three clefs: bass, tenor, and
treble.[1] As with the blue la flashcards, as soon as
Annette realized that there was more than one way
to read the musical staff, and that this depended on
which abstract symbol sat on the left side of it, she
was begging me to teach it to her. Thus she learned
tenor clef when she was six years old. Shortly thereafter, she asked to learn treble clef and thumb position.[2] I finally gave in. She picked it up with the same
lightning rapidity with which she learned to read
books. After that, her practice chart was stuffed with
so many new activities that I wondered how she was
ever going to find the time to continue with the intermediate etudes in bass clef that she still needed

---

[1] The five lines of the musical staff have no intrinsic meaning. The clef sign which is printed on the left side of the
staff is actually an ornate alphabet letter (G for treble
clef, F for bass clef) which indicates that the note name
of that line corresponds with that letter. Once the note
name for one staff line has been fixed, all the others can
be identified simply by counting staff lines and spaces—
up the staff is forward in the alphabet, down is backward.
Learning to read music in different clefs is a complex
task because the note names for the same five lines and
four spaces are different for each clef.

[2] Thumb position is most often used in the upper ranges of
the cello. It is considered an advanced technique. The
left thumb is placed perpendicular to the strings and
stops them (causing a change in pitch) as do the other
fingers. In this capacity it functions somewhat as a capo
does on a guitar.

to help her master that part of the cello. And how did we fit it all into lessons? We couldn't.

But time management is a small problem in educating a profoundly gifted child. It is more difficult yet to locate the proper materials, resources, and educational activities, and it is the ultimate challenge to then perceive the problems that crop up not because you lack these things, but precisely because you have found them. I would never have known any of this if it had not been for the help of our local school district, just about the last place I would have expected to find any support.

But here in Casper, the Natrona County School District No. 1 presently has a self-contained Gifted and Talented classroom. This is a direct result of Linda Silverman's visit to our community in 1998. We have a full time Gifted-Talented facilitator whose job it is to locate eligible students, hire teachers, help parents, and generally support gifted education in the community. This person, Jeanne Spawn, is dedicated to her job, heart and soul.

I began talking with Jeanne when the program was just starting, because I didn't want to rule it out without some investigation. Although we have since chosen to continue home schooling, Jeanne has told me on numerous occasions that she regards it as part of her job to help us. It was through Jeanne that I learned that high school students in our district were sometimes available as tutors. They would do this at no charge, because they would be earning academic credit for it. When I told Jeanne that we were trying to locate a Latin tutor for Annette, she was able to help us find the perfect person. This gifted fourth-year Latin student, Lori Sandercock, visited our house twice a week during the 1999-2000 school year and helped Annette keep pace with the first year Latin class at the high school. She was a perfect match for Annette, and it was an ideal situation. Annette had regular homework assignments, and these, plus the complexity of the subject, forced her to work harder than she has had to work independently at anything except the cello.

We soon discovered that Annette did not have good study habits. Was it due to age, inexperience, or lack of motivation? We didn't know. In our efforts to solve this problem, we had to try many different things. We helped her with her homework, then we didn't help her with it. We sat in on the tutoring sessions and took notes. We instituted rewards and punishments. We discontinued them. We asked her if she really wanted to learn Latin, and she said yes. Somewhere near the end of this stage, we finally realized that we were all traveling up another hump. Annette was learning how to study. We were muddling our way through the tangles of having a young child for whom almost every learning experience had been so easy that rigorous mental activity was almost unknown to her.

I had tried my best with the cello lessons, and Ellis with math, but we often wondered if we had succeeded. At first it appeared to us that Annette was not sufficiently motivated to make it worth Lori's while to work with her twice a week. But then we realized that this was Annette's first extended experience with homework, and perhaps she didn't really know how to handle her study time. We also thought maybe she was a normal six-year-old in some respects, but which ones? Over my years of cello teaching I had participated in so many discussions with parents about their children's practicing, or lack thereof. The comment I had heard most often about children not living up to their potential was, "It's the age." But if that phrase were to fit Annette and her adjustment to the complexities of Latin, to which age would it refer? Chronological? Mental? Emotional? These are the elusive questions for which we must find answers. It is another job for our wits.

During the previous year, our problems were quite different. They were much more serious. We were alone in our efforts to find appropriate educational opportunities for our children. We had no one to discuss this with, and were always scrambling to create the right kind of schoolwork for both Annette and Lewis. Latin instruction has been and will continue to be immensely helpful. Because of it, I can now teach Annette a mundane but necessary skill such as penmanship, so that she can learn to take notes in a classroom, and also so that her writing can fly as fast as her thoughts. Ellis and I can both give more time to Lewis without neglecting Annette. Lori's presence in our lives, and Jeanne's as well, are a fine example of the community serving the needs of a young profoundly gifted child, and thus benefitting the whole family. Given everything I have read in the books, and the history of gifted education, I never thought it could happen. I hope it is the beginning of a nationwide turnaround in gifted education.

We look to the future with hope for ourselves and for Annette and Lewis. Although we have encountered some age discrimination which reveals the world's unreadiness to accept profoundly gifted children, we are not daunted. We do not feel alone in our task any longer. We have finally found the information, and at least some of the resources that our children need. This could be available for more families with gifted children if the supporters of gifted education in every community found each other and began working together.

19

MY MISSION

A final surprise awaited me after I discovered my probable IQ and was in the process of embracing my own oddness. I had a compelling message to bring to the world about the special needs of all gifted people. Writing this book was the least of it.

During the time that I was exploring the possibility of enrolling Annette and Lewis in our local gifted program, I spent hours in conversation with Jeanne Spawn. I began to realize that she and I shared a drive to educate the public about giftedness. Jeanne occasionally taught university courses on gifted education for local teachers, parents, and anyone else who wished to enroll. When she asked if I'd be willing to speak to one of her classes, I consented.

The first time I spoke for an hour, in a question and answer format. I remember feeling guarded because I was still so afraid of publicity and of "coming out of the closet" as a non-eminent profoundly gifted adult. I didn't really know what to say about our children, beyond mention of their IQ range, and commenting that raising them was an isolating experience for Ellis and me.

These few statements kicked off a fascinating discussion. People asked the normal questions: "Before you had your children IQ tested, how did you know they were gifted?" and "What [unusual things] are they doing now?" Of course I had no trouble answering. It seemed to me that this group was unusually receptive. Although some questions revealed a degree of disapproval for our choices, I still handled them well. It was natural that public school teachers would want to know why we were home schooling and why we had traveled to Denver for testing instead of taking advantage of community resources.

Even when someone asked the question that all parents of gifted children have heard one too many times, "But are you giving them the chance to have a normal childhood?" I managed an honest answer that offended nobody. I recalled one of Linda Silverman's comments from Lewis' post-test conference: "If a young child is a musical prodigy, that *is* his childhood; the early single-minded pursuit and mastery of his instrument."

My responses to all of these questions, plus the way in which I participated in the discussion, were a revelation to me. For once I had no trouble keeping track of the dialogue and sticking to the point. In fact, I was more focused and less defensive than I'd ever been. After a long discussion about Annette and Lewis, the questions turned to Ellis and me, and what life was like for us as profoundly gifted adults. My comment was, "It's much easier now that I know who I am!" Jeanne chimed in, "Yes, Becky, you're a lot more relaxed than you were when Linda Silverman was here last year for the conference." I replied, "Yes. I'm a lot happier!"

Jeanne turned to the group and said, "When I first met Becky last year she seemed . . . not very relaxed . . . not exactly a mad scientist type, but intense." From these tactful remarks coupled with my own recollections, I extracted the truth: I *was* a "mad scientist type," and I put people off. I'd attended that conference with a chip on my shoulder; I had no use for the public schools, and my attitude probably stuck out all over me. I was indeed intense, and continually on the defensive.

However, with this group it was the opposite. One woman said, with utter conviction, "Everyone has a mission in life, and yours is clear: to educate people about this important issue." Afterward, a few people thanked me and commented that they had learned a lot.

I drove home thinking about how strange it was to be with people, to talk with them, and not feel alienated afterward. On the contrary, and much to my surprise, I felt a sense of deep satisfaction and fulfillment, even excitement. A few days later, Jeanne told me that I had a profound effect on that group. She said that she knew of three people in particular who had believed that the gifted need no special provisions and, as a result of hearing me speak, had changed their minds. Jeanne actually said that they had become "strongly convinced" that the gifted have special educational needs that must be served.

During the next few weeks I marveled at this unprecedented event: I'd been my usual forthright self, and nobody was offended. Better yet, I'd made an impact beyond anything I could have imagined. I now had clear evidence that I was an effective public speaker on an important controversial issue.

It took me months to adjust to this idea, because I'd spent so much of my life struggling to interact constructively with other people. I was intrigued by this new success, and by the feelings of excitement that accompanied it. Could it be that I had something to offer the world?

Until that point I'd spent my life believing that people's attitudes were entrenched, and that it was no use trying to change anyone's thinking. I had long ago made a personal decision to try not to discuss my opinions with anyone, about a whole spectrum of hotly debated issues. I'd observed that when people disagreed, they didn't usually listen to each other, and that nobody's mind was changed during an argument. However, it appeared that I'd found my cause. I was willing to promote it and to argue in favor of it, even if this meant talking about our children or revealing my own eccentricity.

I began to drop my apologetic attitude about myself without even noticing that I was doing so. Much of the transition occurred while I was revising this book. I'd be rewriting a passage about my giftedness, but without thinking, *Nobody is going to believe this.* I'd expand my descriptions of practicing and writing with no feeling of diffidence, no conviction that I'd be dismissed by readers because of my lack of eminence.

My inner life changed as I began to shed my fixed sense of being a failure. Gradually I ceased to dread the way in which others reacted to me. I didn't realize how far I'd progressed until I spoke to another class, about a year after the first one. My mind was even clearer than before, my answers both searching and on the mark.

I kicked off the two-hour discussion by saying, "Our two children are profoundly gifted and my husband and I are also brilliant. That's Ellis, my introverted husband, at the back of the room. He wanted to be here, but not to have to speak." Then I read several passages from this book about Lewis, Annette, and Ellis. In the midst of the discussion I realized that I was being funny, and more straightforward and self-revealing than I'd ever been.

Where was the opposition? Everyone appeared to be having a good time—and to be learning a lot. I was mystified about this phenomenal level of receptivity, and asked Linda Silverman about it the next time I had the opportunity. She remarked, "Teachers who attend classes on gifted education are probably gifted themselves." I knew from prior reading that one of the symptoms of giftedness is empathy with other gifted people and the desire to advocate for them. This helped to explain the response of the groups to which I spoke.

Of course, I still encounter many people who are opposed to gifted education. As I listen to them, I notice again how much I've changed. When Annette was a toddler and Lewis a baby, and I'd read those library books on giftedness, I cringed from the mere thought of advocacy. I had no inner fortitude with which to meet opposition, and knew that such a battle would devour me.

But now I am not so easily discouraged. I do not avoid conversations about myself, our children, or the special needs of all gifted people. I am not bewildered by my interactions with the world. My personality traits are still natural for me and alien to others, but now I know the reason. I do not have to be chronically on guard, because my clashes with people are no longer mysterious to me. I am not puzzled by answers that make no sense, nor am I drained by feelings of isolation. Best of all, even when I offend someone by speaking clearly and to the point, I do not feel punished.

In discovering my real Self, I have stopped wasting my energy trying to be someone that the world thinks I should be. This change has released a tremendous force within me: the power of a unified mind and spirit. There are certain struggles that I will never have to face again. They are forever vanquished.

APPENDIX A

Characteristics of gifted children:

—Reasons well (*good thinker*)
—Learns rapidly
—Has extensive vocabulary
—Has an excellent memory
—Has a long attention span (*if interested*)
—Sensitive (*feelings hurt easily*)
—Shows compassion
—Perfectionistic
—Intense
—Morally sensitive
—Has strong curiosity
—Perseverant in interests
—Has high degree of energy
—Prefers older companions or adults
—Has a wide range of interests
—Has a great sense of humor
—Early or avid reader (*if too young to read, loves being read to*)
—Concerned with justice, fairness

—Judgment mature for age *at times*
—Is a keen observer
—Has a vivid imagination
—Is highly creative
—Tends to question authority
—Has facility with numbers
—Good at jigsaw puzzles

©Linda Silverman, 1996. Used by permission.
Gifted Development Center
1452 Marion St.
Denver, CO 80218
(303) 837-8378
(888) 443-8331
www.gifteddevelopment.com
gifted@gifteddevelopment.com

APPENDIX B

Characteristics of gifted adults:

—Are you a good problem solver?

—Can you concentrate for long periods of time?

—Are you perfectionistic?

—Do you persevere with your interests?

—Are you an avid reader?

—Do you have a vivid imagination?

—Do you enjoy doing jigsaw puzzles?

—Do you often connect seemingly unrelated ideas?

—Do you enjoy paradoxes?

—Do you set high standards for yourself?

—Do you have a good long-term memory?

—Are you deeply compassionate?

—Do you have persistent curiosity?

—Do you have an excellent sense of humor?

—Are you a keen observer?

—Do you have a love of mathematics?

—Do you need periods of contemplation?

—Do you search for meaning in your life?

—Are you often aware of things that others are not?

—Are you fascinated by words?

—Are you highly sensitive?

—Do you have strong moral convictions?

—Do you often feel out-of-sync with others?

—Are you perceptive or insightful?

—Do you often question rules or authority?

—Do you have organized collections?

—Do you thrive on challenge?

—Do you have extraordinary abilities and deficits?

—Do you learn new things rapidly?

—Do you feel overwhelmed by many interests/abilities?

—Do you have passionate, intense feelings?

—Do you have a great deal of energy?

—Do you often take a stand against injustice?

—Do you feel driven by your creativity?

—Do you love ideas and ardent discussion?

—Were you advanced developmentally in childhood?

—Do you have unusual ideas or perceptions?

—Are you a complex person?

References

Alvarado, N. 1989. Adjustment of Gifted Adults. *Advanced Development* 1:77-86 Denver: Institute for the Study of Advanced Development. Quoting Willings, D. 1980. *The Creatively Gifted: Recognizing and Developing the Creative Personality.* Cambridge: Woodhead-Faulkner.

Delisle, J.R. 1986. *See* Silverman 1993.

Grost, A. 1970. *Genius in Residence.* Englewood Cliffs: Prentice-Hall, Inc.

Harkavy and Asnis 1985. *See* Silverman 1993.

Harvey and Seeley 1984. *See* Silverman 1989.

Hayes and Sloat 1990. *See* Silverman 1993.

Hollingworth, L.S. 1942. *Children Above 180 IQ Stanford-Binet: Origin and Development.* Yonkers-on-Hudson: World Book Company. Reprint. North Stratford, NH: Ayer Company Publishers, 1997.

Kearney, K. 1993. Discrimination Against Excellence. *Understanding Our Gifted* 6 (November/December): 16.

Lovecky, D.V. 1993a. "The Quest for Meaning: Counseling Issues with Gifted Children and Adolescents." In *Counseling the Gifted and Talented,* edited by Linda K. Silverman, 29-50. Denver: Love.

——1993b. Ibid.

——1994. Exceptionally Gifted Children: Different Minds. *Roeper Review* 17 (2): 116-120.

McGuffey's Second Eclectic Reader, Revised Edition 1920. New York: Van Nostrand Reinhold.

Marland, S., Jr. 1972. *See* Silverman 1989.

Perino, S., and J. Perino 1981. *Parenting the Gifted: Developing the Promise.* Serving Special Populations Series. New York: R.R. Bowker.

Silverman, L.K. 1986. Personality Development and the Gifted. *Mensa Bulletin* 299:14-16. Revised 1994.

——1989. The Unmet Needs of Gifted Children. *Kaleidoscope* (January/February): 5-7. Reprinted in 1990 in *Images* 5(1): 8-11; and in 1991, *The G.A.T.E. Post* 2(3): 2-3. Quoting Harvey, S. and K. R. Seeley 1984. An Investigation of the Relationships among Intellectual and Creative Abilities, Extracurricular Activities, Achievement, and Giftedness in a Delinquent Population. *Gifted Child Quarterly* 28:73-79. Quoting Marland, S., Jr. 1972. *Education of the Gifted and Talented.* Report to the Congress of the United States by the U.S. Commissioner of Education. 92d Cong., 2d sess., Washington, DC: U.S. Government Printing Office.

——1993. "Techniques for Preventive Counseling." In *Counseling the Gifted and Talented,* edited by Linda K. Silverman, 81-109. Denver: Love. Quoting Hayes, M.L., and R.S. Sloat 1990. Suicide and the Gifted Adolescent. *Journal for the Education of the Gifted* 13:229-244. Quoting Harkavy, J. and G. Asnis 1985. Suicide Attempts in Adolescence. Prevalence and Implications. *New England Journal of Medicine* 313:1290-1291. Quoting Delisle, J.R. 1986. Death with Honors: Suicide and the Gifted Adolescent. *Journal of Counseling and Development* 64:558-560.

——1995. POGO (Parents of Gifted Offspring) Research Project 160+ Questionnaire. Denver: Institute for the Study of Advanced Development.

——1998. Why Do Gifted Children Need Provisions? Paper presented to Natrona County School District #1 teachers and community members, Casper, Wyoming, August. Revised 2000. "Why Do We Need Gifted Education? A Millennial Perspective." In *Ringing the Bell Curve: Saving and Surviving Amazing Kids* [working title], edited by Kiesa Kay and Annette Revel Sheely. Forthcoming.

Tolan, S. 1996. Is it a Cheetah? Hollingworth Center for Highly Gifted Children. Website: www.hollingworth.org, 5pp.

Willings, D. 1980. *See* Alvarado 1989.